TOMORROW
I'LL BE PERFECT

DAVE STIEB

— with Kevin Boland —

TOMORROW
I'LL BE PERFECT

A Dell Book

Printed and bound in Canada by John Deyell Company
Typesetting by Compeer Typographic Services Ltd.

Canadian Cataloguing in Publication Data

Stieb, Dave
  Tomorrow I'll be perfect

1. Stieb, Dave.   2. Pitchers (Baseball) — United
States — Biography.   I. Boland, Kevin.   II. Title.

GV865.S75A37 1986   796.357'092'4   C86-094044-6

Library of Congress Cataloguing-in-Publication Data

Steib, David, 1957–
  Tomorrow I'll be perfect.

1. Stieb, David, 1957–   .   2. Baseball players —
United States — Biography.   I. Boland, Kevin.   II. Title.

GV865.S785A3 1986   796.357'092'4 [B]   86-13562

ISBN 0-385-25057-6

We gratefully acknowledge the help of the Toronto Blue
Jays in providing statistics.

The book is dedicated to the memory
of my grandparents
John Meeler and Irma Blacker
D.A.S.

For Curlie and Catherine
and Tiny Perfect
K.J.B.

Contents

A Winter of Discontent

The guy from K.C. could call ducks with the best
but all I could hear was the voice of gloom

TIME HEALS EVEN THE WORST WOUNDS, it is said, but what bothers me is that it takes its own sweet time to complete the process.

All this spring and summer, maybe even until the maple leaves turn color in Toronto this fall, I will remember looking over my shoulder and watching a harmless fly ball refuse to drop out of the October night sky. I will remember Jesse Barfield going back, back, back, the spread of his limbs as he climbed the wall in right field at Exhibition Stadium, the dagger deep in my gut when the ball popped off the bar on the top of the fence. I will remember Jim Sundberg of the Royals pumping around first base, the crowd stiffening in disbelief as his bases-loaded triple bounced lazily into a no-man's-land.

Except for flipping the ball to manager Bobby Cox when he came to pull me out of the game a couple of moments later, it was my last pitch of the 1985 season. The Kansas City Royals, as impossible as it had seemed to me a few hours earlier, were on their way to the World Series.

I learned then what it is to die a little.

As much as I tried to banish it from my thoughts, I was reminded of that instant, often at the most curious times: at breakfast, the smell of coffee flooding the kitchen, paper folded at the news of Coxie striking it rich in Atlanta, knowing that I will never see him pull on the uniform again; on the golf course, as I bend over a three-foot putt and grit my teeth as it lips the cup; in the Bronco on the way back from the supermarket, as I turn off the highway and down the street that leads to home, my wife and my youngsters in Palm Harbor, Florida.

Worst of all, of course, was watching the Royals take seven agonizing games to wrap up the World Series. Why, in the name of mercy, couldn't someone have done the job in four or five or six?

One day, channel-hopping on the big screen in the living room, I happened upon a duck-calling contest—yes, a duck-calling contest—and, wouldn't you know it, the winner was from Kansas City. Bullseye. Is there no escape?

Every one of us on this club wondered over the winter how it happened. Who has not had the same bewildering thoughts that I have had? Who does not realize that to dwell on these thoughts invites a madness that could hound us through this season and, perhaps, other seasons? Put it away, we tell ourselves. Learn from it. Be that much better next time.

There has been all sorts of talk of what might have been, if only this or that or the other had been done. I will offer no comment other than to repeat a saying familiar to all who play for keeps:

If we should have won, we would have won.

For the record, however, I will answer the question everyone was asking all winter long. No, despite having pitched three playoff games in nine days, I was not tired. What did me in, if anything, was the stiff wind blowing to right field that night. Had it been in Royals Stadium, even with the same wind, Sundberg's fly would have been a routine out and we would have gone to the dugout down only 2–1. By the same token, I take the blame for allowing Sundberg to come to the plate in such dangerous circumstances. Hitting Hal McRae with a pitch, then walking Steve Balboni, were errors of the first magnitude.

If the experience teaches me anything about the human condition, it is that the mind has no capacity to recall the quality of pain it once knew so vividly. It is as if these things were an out-of-body experience, that they happened to another Dave Stieb, that they were fragments of a dream prompted by the downing of one too many wedges of Boston cream pie at dinner.

At the same time, thanks be to the stars, there is a capacity for total recall of those moments of triumph that ended with the dreadful sound made by Sundberg's bat and the vacuum that sucked up a season of sweat and toil and, yes, tears.

It is an odd comparison, but looking back on it has to be like recalling a raging affair that ended with a lover's betrayal. For the longest time, you remember all that was bad and then, as the psyche chips away at the bitterness, all you recall are the good times you shared.

I am not the first to say this, not by any stretch, but there is much of baseball to be found in life and, conversely, much of life to be found in baseball. What you see between the white lines, you see beyond them. You are born. You struggle. You die. Maybe it takes three score and ten, as the Bible decrees, or nine innings and 125 pitches, as *The Sporting News* says, but it comes out the same sooner or later. I guess what I'm saying is that baseball, like life, is a series of great moments with long pauses in between. And in every season of long pauses, there is one moment, like the North Star on a clear summer night, that stands as a beacon.

October 8, 1985. Game One of the American League

Championship Series. K.C. Royals vs. Toronto Blue Jays at 8:30 p.m., Exhibition Stadium. Dave Stieb (14–13, 2.48) vs. Charlie Leibrandt (17–9, 2.69).

Even with the league's best ERA, I figure my 14–13 record left me with a lot to prove to the legions who doubted me. Win a couple in the next week, win a couple more in St. Louis or L.A. the following week, and no one could doubt the figures were an aberration. On another level, the club was fed up with the "no name" label that had been applied to the "upstart" team from Toronto by the U.S. media. We had won ninety-nine games in the toughest division in baseball, had led it without interruption since May and now, horror of horrors, a Canadian team was threatening to add the prefix "inter" to the national pastime. It was about time we got some respect.

Never had the desire to win, which can achieve the proportions of an inferno in me, been stronger. All of Canada had hopped aboard the bandwagon—the country's prime minister, the Right Honorable Brian Mulroney, was going to throw out the first ball—and anyone who knew a Louisville Slugger from a resin bag had the numbers down pat.

The Royals, particularly Leibrandt, would be tough, no matter how the figures were juggled. His earned run average of 1.79 in four starts (2–0) against us was reflected in our .222 batting average against him. Worse for us, both his wins were complete games at Exhibition Stadium, where his ERA was 1.00 and our batting average .200.

All modesty aside, which I have to admit is one of my most endearing qualities, the guy he would face that night was no bum who had just fallen from his stool at the corner bar and into the Blue Jays' starting rotation.

The Royals had beaten me in each of my three starts against them, but none of the games were gifts. Bud Black had won 2–1 on opening day at K.C. and 4–2 in August. Leibrandt, my opponent in the series opener, shut me out

2–0 in April at Exhibition Stadium. With an ERA of 2.70 and a Royals' batting average of .233, maybe it was my turn to snatch a couple of breaks.

This kind of thinking, as admirable as it might be, was of little comfort that afternoon as I tried to gag down a bologna sandwich at my summer home on the outskirts of Toronto. My wife had gone back to Florida a few days before, to await the birth of Ashley, our second child, early in November, and Bob LaMonte, my friend and agent, had come from California to calm my inclination to climb the walls. I even went so far as to have the workmen report, as they had been doing the past few weeks, to put the finishing touches on the recreation room in the basement.

It was a major effort to make an attempt to convince myself the opener should be treated like a game in the middle of the season. Considering that we won the division on the last weekend of play, considering that the losses in April or June or August all count in October, I found such a state of mind serious enough. It would insult the intelligence of a dribbling idiot, of course, if I said I succeeded in deceiving myself.

As the smell of sizzling bologna filled the kitchen—not all baseball players have worked so diligently to acquire my gourmet's palate—my stomach churned with the thought of what was ahead of me.

No sooner would I divert my thoughts from the game, by doing something brilliant like reading what the newspapers were saying about it, than the prospect flooded back into my mind. When that didn't work, I went downstairs and started hacking away at the Gibson guitar I had picked up during the season. If anything helped me get my head around the immensity of the challenge facing me, it was telling myself it would not be a whole lot different from pitching in the All-Star Game. Since I had pitched in five of them, I pretty well knew what peaks of emotion I would be asked to climb.

For all the mind-bending exercises I had done—or, with great purpose, had not done—I returned to the bench from my warm-up period in the bullpen with an overwhelming sense of confidence. This one, though George Brett would provide a few difficult moments, was in the bag.

The club that had provided me with a grand total of three runs in three outings against the Royals during the season was a distant memory. Sure, we took a peculiar route to scoring a pair in the second inning, but you wouldn't hear me complain. With Jesse Barfield (single to right) and Willie Upshaw (hit by pitch) on base, Garth Iorg popped what looked to be a single into left field. Barfield had to wait to see if the ball would be caught and was forced at third by Lonnie Smith's throw. Oh, oh. Ernie Whitt erased the sinking feeling when he punched a single to right that scored Upshaw and put Iorg on third. Tony Fernandez singled deep to shortstop, sending Iorg home.

We scored three the next inning, one on a walk with the bases loaded, and Leibrandt was gone. We added another in the fourth, when George Bell scampered all the way from first on a hit-and-run grounder by Cliff Johnson and first baseman Steve Balboni's throwing error. It was a feast where there had been famine.

Wouldn't you know it—I pitched as if we didn't have a run to spare. With the war out of the way, I could have a fine time winning all the little battles. None of them, as I state elsewhere in these memoirs, was so entertaining as the confrontation with Mr. Brett.

Georgie walloped a double off the fence in center field with two out in the first inning on a 1-and-2 pitch that ought to have been so far out of the strike zone he would have needed the CN Tower to reach it. Ernie Whitt had called for a fastball way outside, in the faint hope that Brett might go fishing. As my arm reached the top of its arc, I decided to make it a little more inviting. Crack! There goes the perfect game.

Next time up, count 2-and-1, I tried another fastball a little higher in the strike zone. Crack! He drills a single to right-center. There goes the bid for a one-hitter.

Now, after keeping him in the park the first two times I face him, I have to believe I've got him where I want him. (Well, what else is a guy supposed to tell himself?) I mean, slipping a third strike by Brett is about as easy as sneaking the sunrise past a rooster. Still, there are times . . .

It is the sixth inning, we're up six runs and we're sailing. Other than an exotic dancer (translation: stripper) named Juanita who planted a sloppy kiss on my neck as I warmed up for the second inning, the only warm body that had gotten to me all night was Mr. Brett.

Willie Wilson, the fine center fielder, had just gone down on strikes on a checked swing (nice call by the umpire) for the second out of the inning. The look in Brett's eyes, which is the first thing I assess when a hitter settles in, told me he knew it was all over for his club this night, but that he wanted to tear another strip off my hide.

As he would teach us over the next week, to bury the Royals one needed first to bury Brett. Maybe I take too much upon myself, but I have to believe that the Royals felt the same way about me. If Brett could take me downtown—geez, but I like his shave cream commercials—then he and the Royals would salvage a source of no little inspiration from this night.

Damned if I would let him.

I wasted a pitch away, fed him a hard slider inside, wasted another pitch away, then threw him a backdoor slider that looked like it would remain outside, but broke over the plate at the last second. If there is a cardinal rule with Brett, it is that you never show him the same pitch twice because, brilliant hitter that he is, he will jump all over it. With every rule, there are exceptions to be made and this would be one.

Backdoor slider. Again. As soon as I let it go, I knew it

was the pitch of the season. It took hours to get there and, in my mind's eye, I saw myself halfway to the dugout before it crossed the plate. I knew, and it was a feeling that was transmitted to every cell, it would freeze him. He saw it sail to the outside, twigged too late that it was breaking back, flinched as if he had been struck with a bolt of lightning, accepted his fate and wandered out to third base where a teammate brought him his cap and glove.

That night, back home with Bob LaMonte, I swigged champagne and lapped up liver pâté and caviar. From fried bologna sandwiches to an early breakfast of champions, it had been quite a day.

Brett, who singled in the ninth off reliever Tom Henke to go 3-for-4 and do his bit to erase the shutout, also would have his day later. I was blissfully unaware of this fact when my head hit the pillow a couple of hours later and I slipped into dreams of a World Series—dreams that became real the following Saturday night in Kansas City when we slipped by the Royals for a 3–1 lead in the series. It was a classic, even if I did show both sides of my Jekyll-and-Hyde personality on the mound. Though I prevented any damage by Brett and gave up but two hits and struck out six, I walked seven men.

This caught up with me in the sixth inning when Willie Wilson singled to left as Lonnie Smith, whom I had walked to open the inning, was stealing second base. We did the sensible thing by giving Brett a free pass, even though it loaded the bases with none out. Dr. Jekyll gets two quick strikes on Hal McRae, then Mr. Hyde (damn him) throws four straight balls to force in the run. Dr. Jekyll gets Pat Sheridan to pop up the next pitch and induces Frank White to ground into a double play. As miffed as I was to give up the run, I was grateful that the damage wasn't worse.

Though I was gone the next inning, giving way to Tom Henke after walking Buddy Biancalana and Smith, I had this feeling that we would come back. What gave me confidence was a curious thing that happened to me as I walked into the dugout ahead of Bobby Cox. As the jeers and catcalls from the K.C. crowd rose, I felt the elastic start to give way in my athletic supporter. Reflex action, of course, but I had to check if my cup was in place.

Funny, isn't it, how the fans can interpret the most innocent things?

Now, as I look back on it, that triumph of Saturday, October 12, 1985, is tinged with sadness because it was Al Oliver's last hurrah.

In the ninth, after Damaso Garcia walked on four pitches (miracle of miracles) and Lloyd Moseby brought him home with a double to right-center, George Bell blooped a single to center off reliever Dan Quisenberry to put men at first and third with none out.

Oliver, who had delivered the winning run in the tenth inning of our second playoff victory, was doing stretching exercises in the clubhouse when he got the call to pinch-hit for Cliff Johnson. On a 2–0 pitch, a changeup, he looped a double into the right field corner to put us ahead by two.

Henke, with two out and two on (both walks) got pinch-hitter Jamie Quirk on a pop and we were within one game of going to the World Series.

Though the bubbly was on ice, though the first cork had yet to pop, we could taste the pennant. Even champagne, as we discovered on a cold and windswept night in Toronto the following week, can turn to vinegar.

Dammit, but dreams die hard.

Why Me?

Of the 1,250,000 males who graduated with me,
I was the one who got to start in the All-Star Game

I HAVE A SUMMER JOB that pays me roughly a million dollars or, to smooth it out a little, about $225 each time I raise my right arm on the pitcher's mound at any one of fourteen ballparks in the American League.

Why me? Why not my brother Steve?

Steve was the one everybody, myself included, expected to make it. As kids, in high school, in junior college, even as far away as Alaska, the attention was on him and, to be honest, rightfully so. He was that good. Keeping up with him, never mind dreaming about the big leagues, was challenge enough for me.

With the focus on him, I was able to develop in my own way, at my own pace, in my own good time. I had been an infielder in Little League and an outfielder in high school and college, but my only connection with pitching—other than doing my best to hit it—was through Steve. He was the catcher in the family.

The Atlanta Braves saw something in him and, for a couple

of seasons, he played in their minor league system. He had good hands, a good arm and called a smart game. He needed work on his hitting but, to my way of thinking, he was as good as they had on their big club at the time. It nags at me to this day that he didn't make it and I'm sure it hurts him, too. We're close, as close as brothers can be, but it's not the kind of thing we talk about. He's got his own rig now, trucks horses all over California, and shoes 'em, too, when they need it.

Why me? Why not my pal Bob Ash?

We were teammates in high school and junior college and, like thousands of others who catch the eye of a scout, he had the makings of a major leaguer. He was a pitcher at Oak Grove High, good enough to score a four-year ride at Hayward State, but he soon blew out his arm and any chance he had of turning pro. He and his dad make a good living with their roofing company, but like thousands and thousands of others, he has to wonder what might have been.

Why me?

Of the 1,250,000 males who graduate from U.S. high schools each summer, 500 are considered good enough to be offered contracts to play baseball professionally. For that one in 2,500 who might be made of the right stuff, the pay is usually $500 a month. Climbing the four rungs of the ladder to the majors (Rookie, A, AA, AAA) is a process that precious few survive. Our "farm system" is made up of six clubs, ranging from Medicine Hat, Alberta, in the Rookie-Pioneer League to Syracuse, New York, of the International League. That's 150 players, stars in their own eyes, with a shot at two dozen jobs in the big time. There are exceptions, of course, but if they don't make it in three years, they'd better have good career options. Now, look down the roster of the parent club and figure how many will be here when we open the '89 season in our new stadium with the retractable roof. For the sake of argument, let's say the turnover is about fifty per cent (twelve jobs) and that half of the vacancies are filled by trades or signing free agents.

In less than one calendar year, August of '78 to June of '79, I made the jump from Dunedin of the Florida State League (A) to Toronto.

Why me?

With twenty-six teams of twenty-four men in the major leagues—for some curious reason, it was reduced from twenty-five this season—there are 625 jobs available. When you think that there are about 250 of those slots available to a pitcher, you get the idea how long the odds are against a kid from Santa Ana getting the start in an All-Star Game.

Maybe it was in the stars the morning I was born, July 22, 1957, in Santa Ana, California. I am the second son of Peter Andrew Stieb—a big, no-guff sort of guy who wore a hard-hat to work five days a week, and his wife, Patricia Ann. My brother, Steven John, the catcher, reported six weeks late for Opening Day of the '56 season.

I weighed in at 7 pounds, 3 ounces, batted and threw right, stared at the nurse whenever she fumbled my bottle, had no hair on my head and only the tracings of a moustache.

I grew to be 6-foot-1 and 185 pounds, or so the *Official Baseball Register* has been saying for five years, which means I am nothing remarkable as physical specimens go. Kill a few Labatt's Blue Lights after the game, wolf down a few sides of pork ribs, knock off too many steak fillets on the road and, like lots of folks who hate pushing away from the table, I start looking for the little weasel who's been monkeying with the bathroom scales. Modesty never having been among my many faults, when I maintain there are others whose talent and abilities compare with mine, it is the truth. I could list names by the dozen, good players who made their marks and were gone, who must wonder what they did to deserve so brief a fling.

Why me?

For sure, the Toronto club was not concerned that I was about to tear down the fences, as short as they were, at Exhibition Stadium. I was their fifth choice, 106th over-all, in the free agent draft of 1978. I was an outfielder, with decent power and an exceptional arm, but I had never tossed a competitive pitch until I played for Southern Illinois University—and then only in emergencies.

The way I hear it, the club sent super scouts Bobby Mattick and Al LaMacchia to take a look at the shortstop on the Eastern Illinois team against whom we were playing a double header. As so often happens on a shopping expedition, they didn't buy what they had in mind when they went there. A number of times that season, because of a shortage of pitchers, I came in from the outfield to toss a couple of innings. Why it had to happen that day I have no way of knowing, but what Mattick and LaMacchia saw they must have liked. A lot.

The following summer, after nineteen games (128 innings) in the minors, I was in Baltimore the evening of June 26, 1979. I was all of twenty-one years old and, even if the Orioles did pound me 6–1, I was pitching in the big leagues. And for big money, too. I made $19,000 that year.

Why me?

Maybe it's the difference between wanting something and needing it.

Call it pride. Call it confidence. Call it arrogance. In baseball, I learned quickly, the meek inherit the earth, six feet by three feet by six feet. Humility, and we're not talking about the guff a hitter spouts the night he goes 5-for-5, is for losers.

Next time you see a bunch of kids kicking up dust on a sandlot, stop for a couple of minutes and, pretty soon, it becomes apparent which one is the best. Not necessarily the biggest, the fastest, or the one with the most talent. He's the one who needs it the most and, as important, the one with the pride, the confidence, the arrogance to see that he gets it.

What can be seen on that sandlot is what can be seen, no less and no more, on the manicured fields of the major leagues. If somebody can be the best, then I have to wonder why it can't be me. And since no one holds the patent on that notion, there is no limit to the number of players on a team who can think it, act upon it, make it come true. With this type of grit on a club, although there is room for only one to be the best, the whole adds up to much more than the sum of the parts.

In my heart of hearts, do I believe I am the best? A resounding yes. Doyle Alexander and Jimmy Key think they're the best, too, and last season their won-lost records reflected it. Dennis Lamp, the reliever the fans nearly ran out of town in '84, was merely perfect in long relief at 11-0 and, deservedly, was named the club's top pitcher. Coming out of spring training last April, I still felt it would be me. To be honest, I'd be bothered if Alexander, Key, Jim Clancy and everyone else on the team did not think the same of themselves. I wouldn't have it any other way.

Just in case anyone thinks that I increase my hat size at the start of each season — some people think this happens every time I am issued a uniform — I might remind them that of all games, baseball is the most humbling to those who think they've conquered it. Hitters proud of their .300 average are all too aware that it also reflects a .700 failure rate. What good is the best earned run average in the league (2.48) when it only produces a won-lost record of 14-13? The ERA title is nice, thank you, but it does not win a division title, a pennant, a World Series or even a Cy Young Award for you. The name of the game is victories.

Over the years, baseball has changed me, has taught me some important lessons. I look at all those great little kids who come to the games in wheelchairs, their eyes alight and smiles beaming, and wonder what wondrous thing I ever did to be where I am today. As I loaf in the outfield during batting practice, I see mom, pop and the kids trooping into the bleachers. Four tickets at four dollars apiece, treats for everyone, parking. I think about how hard my dad worked for his money and the contract I have with those families when I cash my paycheck. I think of how a city and a country, in which none of the players on this team were born, took us to their hearts.

What can I say that would begin to measure up?

I know, too, that there is another side of me that people see. There but for the grace of God goes God. The only guy in the major leagues who can strut when he's sitting on the bench. Hi, I'm Dave Stieb and you're not. On those rare occasions when my cap gets a little tight on my swelled head, all I have to do is think about what happens on the field. I know hitters, lots of them, who went 0-for-5 in an afternoon or two, but how about starting a season 0-for-April and most of May as I did this year?

The truth of it is that compliments make me nervous. When someone walks up to me and says I'm one of the best pitchers in baseball, how do I respond? Agree and I'm full of myself. Disagree and, to be honest, I'm full of something else. I guess a simple thank-you would suffice, but the social graces never came gracefully to me. It's when people tell me I'm something more than a pitcher, however talented, that I really begin to squirm. So my face is on TV or in the sports pages, does that make me a better human being than a teacher, a punch-press operator, a policeman? Not to my mind.

Because a pitcher spends most of his existence examining his inner self—most intensely on the days before, during and after a game, more so when he loses—he tends to be an insular type. If he learns to express himself, it is usually in the area of what he does best. Pitching a baseball past a man with a big stick comes as close to being primitive, without drawing 3-to-5 in the state pen, as a human is legally allowed to be. There are times when I'm sure the game's roots were planted when one cave man slung a rock and another put his club to it. It makes more sense, come to think of it, than dropping bombs.

On a given night, when I pitch to my capacity and win, I feel that I did what I do best better than anyone in the world that day. When things go the other way, the depths are just as intense. With a career record of 95–80 heading into the '86 season, the good nights slightly outnumber the bad in the seven years I have been here.

Sure, the money is great.

Product of the middle class that I am, I never dreamed I would make a million dollars in my lifetime, much less in a single year. It's ridiculous when you work it out on a dollars-per-pitch basis. Multiply thirty-five starts by an average 125 pitches for a total of 4,375 in a season. Divide it into $1 million and it comes to $228.57 on the cash register every time I wind up.

As unlikely as it sounds to anyone trying to make ends meet, the money means nothing to me the moment I cross the white line on my way to the mound. Money is for the real world, an insurance policy for when my time is done, a guarantee of freedom to do what I want, where I want and with whom I want. It is everyman's dream and, for me, it just happened to come true.

It also entails responsibilities that, to tell the truth, complicate a life that needs no more complications. The sports pages are littered with stories of athletes who had it all and then, pardon the expression, pissed it away. I pay my bills and I have bought myself some nice toys, thank you, but I never was one to squander money. Still—and it is a harrowing experience I will detail in this book—I understand how a man and his earnings can be parted.

I have faith that I would have been happy without the money coming my way, but I often wonder if I would have been happy without being able to play this game. Whether it be for a factory club on Sundays or in the most splendid stadiums man has built as monuments to baseball, I think I could have settled for either so long as I was certain I had made the most out of my abilities.

I wonder what it will be like when I can play no longer, a thought that leaves me with an empty feeling. Like any athlete, I will die twice. The first time will be when my eyes or my arm or my legs give out; the next time when they put me in a box and shovel dirt over my head.

Every summer, I get a premonition of what that first demise will be like when I see the television clips from the Hall of Fame ceremonies at Cooperstown. Almost always, the inductee will say it is the happiest day of his life, but I'll bet he would trade it all if he could go back to his prime for one more afternoon at the yard. I would be proud to join them one day, no question, but if they're so happy, then why do they cry?

They say you never miss something until you don't have it anymore, but I don't think that's true. Some day, too soon for my liking, I will find out. Maybe then I will have the answer to the question, Why me?

All in the Family

We'd explore mountain caves and capture turtles
but desert scorpions and angry rattlers were safe

THE ROAD.

Baltimore, Boston and Cleveland. Detroit, Milwaukee and New York. Anaheim, Arlington and Chicago. Kansas City and Minneapolis. Oakland and Seattle.

Like a kid sprung from school for the summer, I could not get enough of the new found sense of freedom that travel afforded me that first summer I spent trucking across North America with a team on the big league baseball circuit.

All the stops—yes, even Cleveland—held a fascination for me those days. Anaheim and Oakland, because they brought me back to my California roots. Seattle for its big, blue skies. Baltimore and Boston for the sights and good grub. Chicago and Minneapolis for shopping. And New York is a rush. Well, I'm sure you get the picture even though I forgot to send a postcard.

Just as it is with a steady diet of anything, I'll bet that even London and Paris and Rome wear thin with repetition. So it is with me, after seven seasons inspecting every airport on the American League circuit. Sure, scoffers say that we get up to all kinds of tricks away from home, but it just isn't the case.

The high point of the day is lunch, believe it or not, but even then you have to be careful not to eat anything that will rumble during the game that night.

Among the favorite ways of killing an afternoon on the road are touring department stores, answering fan mail, catching a movie or another installment of a favorite soap opera (mine is "All My Children"), or taking a nap you might not really need.

I don't know how I stand the pace.

The team bus leaves for the stadium at 5 o'clock and if it is only half-full, it is because the rest of the guys were so bored that they are already at the ballpark.

Before and after batting practice, we play cards. Pluck and Hearts, games that are based on suits and the taking of tricks, are to ballplayers what Old Maid and Snap are to kids. It is about the only time in life when losing can be nearly as much fun as winning. Jim Acker and I were partners against Bill Caudill and Gary Lavelle in a Pluck tournament that lasted the entire '85 season. Acker is the kind of player who can remember every card laid down, which is a major advantage in games like Hearts and Pluck where the entire deck is played. When we lose, as we sometimes did, Acker would stomp away from the table muttering curses that would curdle the milk of a Texas rattler. It cheered me up to know that I could ruin his day with the turn of a single card.

When the ballgame is done and we've taken the bus back to the hotel, it's nearly midnight and, finally, time to get loose. The problem is that anybody with a shred of sense is soon fast asleep.

The remaining options are wolfing down the meal most men my age had with their families six hours before; or, if one cannot bear the thought of sleeping on a bloated stom-

ach, firing off a 21-beer salute to the morning sun. Both
choices, experience has taught me, are about as much fun as
watching re-runs of Love Boat.

To be honest, and it sounds like so much chocolate syrup
to anyone but a travelling salesman, the first thing I do upon
returning to my luxurious home away from home is call my
wife and give her the third degree about the wild times she
and the two kids are having while I'm away.

It does not surprise me that I have become a family man
or that, very much the case on this club, I am far from being
alone. If I could have cornered the concession on baby gifts
last season, I might not have had to work so hard on making
bonus clauses. Every other week I seemed to be carting pack-
ages wrapped in pink or blue through the clubhouse doors.
My timing, of course, was impeccable. A couple of weeks
after the season was done, Pattie gave birth to Ashley, our
second child, first daughter. If necessary, I will not hesitate
to drop a series of subtle hints throughout the '86 season.

Often, on the nights this summer when I am far from my
home on the outskirts of Toronto, I will think about all that I
am missing. I'm not complaining, really. I have no right,
considering the fine things this game has put on my table.
Still, I remember what it was like for me when I was growing
up and what it meant to know that my parents would be there
when I got home.

I remember summers spent in the family's one-room
cabin, framed by the yucca trees of the Joshua Tree National
Monument, nestled in the San Bernardino Mountains on the
southern flank of the Mojave Desert.

During the day, Steve and I would wander through the
rocks, explore our favorite caves, catch lizards and turtles,
give the widest of berths to scorpions and rattlesnakes. We
would bury bottles of soda pop in the ground, wait for them
to cool and, when we returned parched from our travels, guzzle them while we inhaled the sandwiches mom had made us

that morning. At night, before we went to bed, we would search for stars in the desert sky and watch the twinkling lights of Palm Springs, another world away.

The developers discovered it a few years back and now, where I once had a youngster's free rein, there are swarms of people, row upon row of houses and ribbons of pavement nailed down by light poles. I know now a little of what the Indians and the mountain men must have felt a century or so ago when "civilization" began to crowd them out.

I guess, too, we were part of that civilization.

We lived in Yorba Linda, about ten miles northeast of Anaheim (where the Calfornia Angels play) on a street of families with growing kids. Like my father, the men made livings through nothing less exalted than hard work. My dad was a contractor — patios, walkways, foundations and the like. He and my mom had an abiding interest in the games we played, which happened to be whatever was in season, from the time we got home until the light was gone. With appropriate breaks for dinner and homework, of course, though truth forces me to say we were anything but scrupulous in observance of these latter two rites.

So far as I can tell, we were no different from any other kids who grew up in any other middle-class neighborhood. In other words, if I had a dollar for every time my mom said, "Wait till your dad gets home," I could have retired long before I decided to take up pitching for a living. My brother and I were always in trouble and paternal retribution, by way of a wooden slat three inches wide and eighteen inches long, was dispensed if and when he was able to catch us.

We had dogs, a beagle we named Baby and a boxer with an uneven temper we called Dino. We had a turtle named Myrtle that we found one day by the railway tracks and who is still part of the family. We had rabbits in a hutch and some nights we could go to sleep owning but a pair of them and wake up the next day with half a dozen more, tiny though they might have been.

Into each life, we also learned, some tears must fall.

After one of these multiplication lessons, which occurred in a burrow Mother Rabbit had fashioned hastily in the backyard, Dino reverted to his baser instincts and taught us a brutal lesson in subtraction. For once, my father's ire was diverted to the canine branch of the family.

I remember another time, painfully, how one of the furry little critters got into my father's lumber yard and, as a result of injuries to his extremities—even today, I have to cross my legs at the thought of it—had to be put to sleep. To waste not was to want not, the family felt, but there was no way I could partake of dinner that night, no matter how much the rest of them told me how close the taste was to broiled chicken, which is a favorite of mine.

Except for breaking an ankle sliding into the mud at third base in my second year of high school, there were no broken bones to record in the family archives. There were, however, harrowingly close calls.

In the summers before we moved from Yorba Linda to San Jose, a place where my father was able to find steadier work, we spent most of our days at the beach and most of the time body-surfing on waves that could peak at twelve feet. I thought my number was up one day when I was sucked into the curl of one breaker. Round and round I tumbled, arms and legs flailing, not knowing which way was up or how far was down. When I hit, I exploded upwards and it seemed like hours before I broke the surface and my lungs sucked in gallons of air.

Champagne, of which I have had my share, never tasted so sweet.

And, ahhh, how empty youth would have been without

knowing the raptures of emotion dismissed by the adult as puppy love. It was in Grade 7, I think. Her name makes no difference now, but let me say that to confirm the depth of my feeling, I had to give her a ring. I was sure, as sure as I am of a backdoor slider catching a corner, that my mom would not miss one of the sparklers in her jewelry box in the bedroom. As I would discover in later years with the slider, I learned then that confidence is not all that it is cracked up to be.

Other guys, I am sure, would have cooked up a dilly of a story for the girl, but not Mr. Honest. "Hey, hon, my mom kind of found out about the ring I took and I have to give it back." She was more than a little upset with me but, prizing honesty more than tact, forgave me. To this day, I hope life has been good to her. Whatever, I am sure she can sympathize with the latest (and last) love of my life.

I met Pattie at a place called And Chili, the restaurant where she worked, on her twenty-first birthday. From the very moment I saw her, I knew I was in trouble and, although there have been times when she has denied it, she was, too.

She had opinions about any number of things, still does, and my status as a "celebrity" counts for absolutely nothing on those rare occasions when we have one of our "discussions."

We were married on August 14, 1981, at Toronto's City Hall and, nine months later to the day, we had Andrew David. He is a stubborn little fellow and, when he has a certain look in his eye, there is nothing short of a tank that can stop him from doing mayhem. In this respect, he must take after his mother.

In all seriousness, I have every respect for her and the lot in life the fates have cast for her. Admittedly, material benefits are something for which we are thankful. We know, having come from middle-class backgrounds, what it takes for parents to house and clothe a family, to put food on the table. Still, it is not easy for her.

With me, she travels the five-day cycle that marks my profession as a starting pitcher in the major leagues. She shares in the elation and in the dejection, but where I have a hand in determining these feelings, all she can do is stand by and wait.

For three months every summer, and particularly last year when she waited for the birth of our second child, she must get by on her own. After every spring training, after every season's end, she must move from home to home, house to house. Some wives tend to be more outgoing and enjoy the celebrity associated with the lives of their athlete-husbands; others, perhaps more introspective, struggle to tolerate them. For Pattie, a woman supremely content to spend an evening around a fire in the hearth, the attention tends to be a strain.

No one said it would be easy, I am all too aware on nights when I slip between the sheets in a strange hotel room in a strange city, but no one could have told me how hard it can be.

Ballplayers may not be allowed to cry, but they sure as hell can get homesick.

Opportunity Knocks

*Pat Gillick and my future were at the door
and I found out how a condemned man feels*

AS MOMENTOUS EVENTS GO, the first time I hauled on the uniform of a major league team was, strictly speaking, something less than memorable.

You would think, for a kid who had just turned twenty-one years old, that every detail of the occasion would be burned into his memory. It ought to be something that, even if he did no more than toss a few lukewarm fastballs on the sidelines, he could tell his pals, his children and his children's children.

It probably will come back to me some day, the way old pitching coaches tend to remember every last lick of what happened on a Sunday in St. Louis a hundred years ago, but it's all a haze to me now. Maybe it's like what happens to some people in car crashes. Everything up to a certain point is as clear as crystal, but the moment of impact draws nothing but a blank.

I cannot recall a single face in the clubhouse that summer day I drove from my parents' home in San Jose to the Oakland Coliseum where this team from Toronto, on a swing through the West Division of the American League, wanted a closer look at the hot prospect they had made their fifth choice (106th overall) in the free agent draft.

There was big money at stake. I wanted $35,000 to sign. Why I picked thirty-five Gs is a mystery, but for some reason the number appealed to me. Their last bid was $22,000 and a car—not a Cadillac, mind you, but something more than four wheels and a board.

Not that any of this mattered. At that particular moment I was doing my best impersonation of the invisible man in the Toronto clubhouse. I was too interested in setting a world record for changing out of street clothes and into a hand-me-down uniform to notice who might be a future teammate. How I tied the laces, whether I had my spikes on the proper feet, what number I wore, these are details that history may never record.

I can't remember the walk to the bullpen in right field and I think, though I can't swear to it, that among the faces waiting for me there were manager Roy Hartsfield and pitching coach Bob Miller. Bob Davis, I have been told, did the catching.

I was wishing I was back in Alaska.

I was playing center field up there for the Kenai Oilers. I got the job, oddly enough, when Rick Leach went back to the University of Michigan for football camp. I was all set to return after the summer to Southern Illinois University for my senior year with the Salukis.

As part of the deal with the Oilers, one of four teams in the semi-pro Alaskan league, we spent a week loafing in the Pacific and playing against the University of Hawaii baseball team. I was there that June when my parents called to tell me I had been drafted. My first thought was that compulsory military service had been discontinued. When they told me it was the Toronto ballclub, my first two questions were, "Who? Where?"

A cursory check with some of my teammates on the Oilers provided a few sketchy impressions of a city I was only vaguely aware had a team in the major leagues of baseball. The streets were clean and you could walk them at night. Almost to a fault, the fans of the Toronto club were polite— remember, this was 1978, long before they started selling beer at the ballpark—but they were nuts about baseball, even if there was a suspicion they had seen it played only by visiting teams. True, after nine months of winter, there were three months of poor skating, but could it be all that different from an Alaskan summer? Besides, 106th draft choices—no matter how good they might think they are—don't control the market.

Still, we make do with what we have.

I remember my first major-league chuckle. It was when they offered me $7,500 to sign and $500 a month to play for the Dunedin Jays of the Florida State League. Hell, you can't blame a guy for trying. Well, then, how about $9,000? Nice try, but I had run out of cigars. Kenai, here I come.

Wayne Morgan, one of the club's top scouts, showed up in Alaska and, after a couple of weeks of discussion, the offer was up to $22,000 and a mid-size Oldsmobile. I wanted my $35,000 and, although I knew there would have to be some give on my part, $13,000 (car or no car) was too much. I was driving a hard bargain.

Then came the offer to pay the tab for a trip home to San Jose around the time the Toronto club would visit Oakland. Without the prospect of more money, I told them, there would be little point travelling all that way for what, in essence, amounted to a workout. Their argument (home cooking, assessment by major league personnel, a hint of movement on money) swayed me. Talk is cheap, no offence intended, but money talks.

Since the club had been good enough to show interest, it was necessary for me to reciprocate the good faith. I wanted to give them no reason not to draft me next time. Richard

"Itchy" Jones, my coach at SIU, believed another season with the Salukis could lead to being chosen in the first round the following June. Why get on the wrong side of a potential employer, I thought, particularly one who seems to have a decided interest. Baseball is a small family and I didn't want word getting around that I was an impossible child. Still, I wanted whoever drafted me, whether this year or next, to think I would deal as hard with them as I would work for them.

The club had thoughts of converting me to a pitcher and, to be candid, my experience was minimal. I still think I could have made it as an outfielder, but there was a certain amount of risk on their part. The workout went pretty well, as far as I was concerned, and they said they liked what they saw. Then again, what else were they going to say? "Hey, kid, you're a stiff. Why not try it with the glove on the other hand?"

I went home and did a pretty good job of persuading myself it wouldn't make that much difference if they never called. The way I looked at it, another year at the university would accomplish at least two things. My education would be completed and, with a little more concentration on pitching, I would know much more about the direction my pro career should take.

At the time, I could hardly assess my chances as a pitcher. Since I could put nine of ten fat pitches across the plate, my teammates behaved like dogs in heat when I took the mound for batting practice. Not a good sign. I had worked a little relief for the Salukis that season and on one occasion, I started a game. The orders were to pitch four innings and, if we were ahead, hand the ball over to a starter looking to pad his record for the scouts. On the plus side, "Itchy" (I never asked how he came by that name) settled on me for spot duty after pitching coach Mark Newman tested the outfielders' arms in the bullpen. After showing me twice how to throw the slider, Newman told Jones mine was the best on the staff.

Just look at the numbers and you can imagine the quandary I faced. In my last season as a college outfielder, I hit .394 with 13 home runs had 48 RBIs, and was named the team's most valuable player. As a part-time pitcher, I had given up two earned runs in the only seventeen innings I had ever pitched. Another year at SIU, I kept telling myself, would do nothing but benefit me.

There was a knock at the door.

It was Pat Gillick, Bobby Doerr, the former Red Sox great who was now a hitting instructor for the Toronto club, and the familiar Wayne Morgan. True to Gillick's nature, he came quickly to the point. How much, he wanted to know, would it take to sign me?

Push had come to shove.

I figured I could get more than twenty-two Gs, particularly if I had a good season in my senior year at SIU. I knew they wouldn't accept my favorite number, thirty-five. I don't know why, but twenty-eight sounded right.

They left, saying they had to consult higher powers in Toronto, but would be back a little later. Again, I put my emotions on hold and, if I do say so, did a fair job of it. Until the next knock on the door.

Somehow, I knew my life was at a major turning point. If Gillick had been given the green light, my fate was sealed. Meet the figure I had set and, as good as my word, I was theirs. As I walked across the living room carpet toward the door, I got an idea how the condemned man feels when they slip the hood over his head.

I opened the door. Pat Gillick came through, his hand extended. "We've got a deal," he said. I can't remember signing the contract. I came down off cloud nine a couple days later when I reported to Grant Field in Dunedin—at the time, not what I would consider the pearl of minor league parks—for my first pro season, however brief it would be.

I was 2–0, gave up twenty-three hits in twenty-six innings, ten runs (four unearned) and had an ERA of 2.08. Not bad, I figured, and in the truest traditions of free trade, I also figured I was due for a raise. Good thing they never mentioned the 35 games I played in the outfield, but everybody knows pitchers aren't supposed to hit. I had kept the faith by batting .192, but I did have seven assists.

Beginning with the 1979 season, I would make $550 a month with the Dunedin Jays, with more to come. Geez, I felt proud. By mid-season, my record was 5–0 with an ERA of, ugh, 4.24, but it was good enough to earn me a promotion to the Syracuse Chiefs of the International League (AAA), one step removed from the majors, and a raise to $900 a month. A couple of weeks later, I went into the Chiefs' head office and after a little head-knocking, squeezed out another $100 a month. High finance. It was almost as good as winning, which I also did to the tune of 5–2 with a 2.12 ERA.

After 128 innings in the minor leagues and a record of 12–2, I made my major league debut in Baltimore on June 26, 1979. The Orioles, apparently, took no notice. They trashed me 6–1 and, without going into gruesome detail, I could no longer boast that I had never given up a home run or two.

I finished with an 8–8 record, which is not bad, a 4.33 ERA, which is, and had seven complete games to prove I could take my punishment.

Back home in California, I added up the take. For a kid who had not worked a day that year—baseball not being exactly what I considered hard labor—I had done very well. By my reckoning, I had made almost $20,000 and had been smart enough to keep most of it.

When an agent came knocking on the door that winter, telling me there was much more to be had, I was all ears. That was one time, though it took me nearly three years to find out, that I would have been better off if I hadn't been home.

Dollar Daze

For a guy winning his share on the field
I was taking a financial beating off it

FOR FIVE CENTS ON THE DOLLAR, you can get someone to do your dirty work for you. And, if it is done the right way, by the right person, at the right time, it can be a bargain.

It is why, not to be too cute about it, the budding professional baseball player hires a business agent. It is also why he should be cautious in the extreme about whom he chooses to oversee his financial affairs.

I did the first. I did not, at least to my mind, do the second.

So, although the story I am about to unfold tends to embarrass me a little, if it spares another fresh-faced kid some of the grief that came my way, then telling it will have served some purpose.

A few details are in order before we examine the events of that day in February 1980 that were to cause me, the team's front office and our followers so much anxiety over the next few years.

In the time it had taken me to pitch 128 innings "down on the farm," my fortunes had risen from that of a virtual unknown to one of baseball's most promising performers.

With an 8–8 record after half a season in the majors, I believed I fulfilled the fondest hopes of a club that drafted me 106th over-all in the June '78 draft. I believed then, as I do now and as I will tomorrow, that there was much more and much better to come.

Only Tom Underwood, who was 9–16 for the entire season, had won more games than I did for a team that lost 109 times and finished last in the East Division, 50½ games behind the leader. I had earned $19,000 for the three months' work, based on the major-league minimum salary of $38,000 a season.

The team and I agreed I deserved much more in '80. The difference was in our interpretations of what "much more" meant. What I felt should have been a gap in our appraisals turned out to be more of a chasm when the mailman delivered the club's proposal a couple of weeks before Christmas.

Steve Comte, an agent based in San Francisco, had been in touch with me that winter and suggested we talk about my need for representation. Early in February, a couple of weeks before I would report to spring training, he visited me at my parents' home in San Jose.

Comte believed he could get me $75,000 to $85,000 for my first full season in the majors. For a number of reasons, he suggested, it would be unwise of me to undertake my own contract talks. Chief among these reasons, of course, is that personal relations can be strained when managers, as they must, try to get the most for their money and the player, as he must, tries to get the most for his services.

Comte had made his point. I just hoped it was all going to work out.

Since he had negotiated other pro contracts and since I wanted nothing off the field to complicate what happened to me on it, I signed a one-year deal with my first agent. If, for any reason, his efforts failed to satisfy me, I could end our contractual relationship by giving him written notice at least thirty days before any subsequent anniversary of the signing of the agreement.

Comte however, was unable to persuade the club that I was worth the $75,000 to $85,000 we suggested and I was left with the impression that the club was grasping, miserly, and tight-fisted and didn't think much of me as a person and a player.

Until I had two years' service in the major leagues—changed to three in the agreement the union negotiated with the owners in 1985—the club had the right to renew, automatically, my contract at a figure they deemed fair. After two years, I could opt for binding arbitration if we did not agree to terms.

The club, arguing I had spent only three months in the major leagues, settled on $55,000 for the '80 season. While I was upset with an organization that had been touting me as one of the hired hands who would lead it out of the wilderness, I also began having doubts about whether I had the right agent.

With a little finesse, I wondered, could he have bumped their $55,000 another $10,000? In hindsight, maybe I should have considered that making $17,000 more than a minimum $38,000 would hardly shame me when I took the checks to the bank. Nevertheless, at five per cent of $55,000, I had paid Comte $2,750 and change and the only result evident to me was that I was at odds with my employer.

As I have said, Comte had certain gifts as a communicator. I figured that, at the very least, he deserved a second chance. I gave him good numbers to work with—my record in '80 was 12–15 (3.70 ERA), second only to Jim Clancy, 13–16 (3.30). We figured that $100,000 to $110,000 was not out of line. The club renewed my contract (big surprise) at $85,000.

Comte and I figured I was being shafted. If I was one of the building blocks of a team with a glowing future, then why was I being paid—compared with some of the guys I had to pitch against—like the water boy on a construction site? Just wait till next year, my first chance to go to arbitration, and then it would be my turn to get even.

This is not conducive, I hardly need say, to harmonious relations between a young pitcher and a club that was beginning to reach respectability. I was in a bad situation. The club wasn't budging, and nor was I. But they were in the better position. Looking back on it, perhaps if we had been more flexible things may have turned out to my advantage.

Either way, the bottom line was that Comte was now 0-for-2 and our adversaries, a term that typified the relationship precisely, were pitching a shutout.

During the strike-shortened '81 season, I had become the first pitcher in the club's history to post a winning record (11-10, 3.18 ERA). There was no question in my mind that I deserved a lot more than the "conservative" contracts I had been awarded after other seasons.

There were other, important personal considerations. On August 13, 1981, I was married at Toronto's Old City Hall and, as the '82 season approached, we were anxiously awaiting the baby that would arrive in mid-May. Now, for the first time in my life, I would be responsible for three people. Although I was twenty-four years old, head of a family, had unlimited prospects and, therefore, had every reason to be happy, all was not what it might have appeared to be. If some weird stroke of fate befell me in the next few months—I wouldn't have been the first to have been cut down in his prime by a freak injury—where would the family be without a document that guaranteed me a certain sum for services about to be rendered? I would have been on the street, that's where, scrambling for work that would allow us to make ends meet.

For thousands who come to the ballpark each night, this is a hard reality. I have a clear idea of what it is like. My parents work hard, have done all their lives, for the same reasons as ninety-nine out of one hundred people in the stands. A decent home. Supper at six o'clock with the family. A night out with the boys/girls once in a while. I might kick around figures in the hundreds of thousands of dollars, but I do not think anyone truly begrudges me all I can get. I have a (perishable) product. I spare no effort to improve it. The way I see it, a lot of people are attracted to the park by the way I pitch, so I deserve a fair share of the profits. Retirement in this job does not come at sixty-five. It could come as soon as the next pitch.

We set our sights on $350,000. The club offered $210,000 with $40,000 to $50,000 in incentives. For some reason, we could not come to terms. Next stop, binding arbitration: each side submits one figure, with no provisions for bonuses or incentives. The club offered $250,000. I wanted $350,000. No longer, however, was it a matter of dollars. Competitive as I am, after two losses in negotiations, I could not bear the thought of being beaten at the bargaining table three years in a row. Guess who lost.

For a guy who was about to make roughly $7,500 for every afternoon he worked, I was one unhappy fellow. Something was very wrong, I figured, and as much as I hate to make such admissions, perhaps Dave Stieb and company ought to look at their own performance.

For three seasons, Comte had been employed by me to negotiate contracts. He was now, for whatever reason, 0-for-3 and the club's shutout remained intact. I had paid him five per cent of roughly $400,000, or close to $20,000, and I could not see where I was any further ahead. As can be the case with other agents, there had been no financial planning, no endorsement deals had been made, no opportunities had been seized to take advantage of a period of peak earning capacity. The Canadian taxman and Uncle Sam were taking their maximum bite because I knew nothing about shelters and other methods of spreading out my responsibilities.

During that summer, I came to the conclusion that I would part company with Comte, as per our agreement that I give him written notice of termination thirty days before the contract's anniversary. I figured that the proper thing to do in such a situation would be to advise him promptly of the action I intended to take. He was astonished by my decision but, since I was resolved to make the break, there was nothing he could do about it. Or so I thought.

It was around this time that I signed a few autographs that would end up costing me $125,000 in hard cash and months of worry. As smart as I like to think I am and as extenuating as circumstances might have been, I still find it difficult to believe I acted so unwisely.

Letters of the Law

On paper, I had two agents acting on my behalf
but I didn't want either one working for me

NO WONDER I'M NOT all that eager when it comes to signing autographs—a couple of them came close to costing me $1.5 million.

That they would set me back a nickel, never mind $125,000 in legal fees, is something I will never forget.

About six weeks into the '82 season, around the time I decided I would have to replace Steve Comte as my business agent, Lemanczyk visited the team's clubhouse in Yankee Stadium to renew acquaintances.

One of the few members of that first expansion club who lived up to the billing as a major leaguer, he had been traded to the California Angels for pitcher Kenny Schrom midway through the '80 season. Finished as a pitcher, Lemanczyk was scouting for the New York Yankees and, as coincidence would have it, had an interest in a firm known as Players Management Associates Inc.

I told him of my concerns regarding the high rate of tax I had been paying on my earnings. Every dime that accrued to me had been exposed to the tax departments of two countries.

One need not be a Paul Beeston, the financial whiz-bang who can tell you to the last Labatt's Blue Light bottle cap how a baseball team can draw nearly 2.5 million fans and still lose money, to realize that there are ways of easing the government's bite. It can be as simple as putting a few bucks into a hamburger stand or as fancy as setting up an annuity that, activated at age thirty-seven, pays twenty annual installments of $500,000 until the investor can begin collecting his pension at age fifty-seven.

In Toronto a couple of weeks later, I met Lemanczyk and his partner at an office downtown to discuss my tax burden. Believe it or not, the next thing I knew, I was signing something that could make Lemanczyk my agent when and if I severed my relationship with Comte. I also signed, with the same stipulations, forms that could be sent to the club and to the Major League Players' Association identifying Lemanczyk as my agent.

Why was I signing something that, on the surface, would tie me to Lemanczyk's firm when I was still under contract to Comte until the following February?

Good question.

It didn't matter that I would never use Comte's services again, that I had informed him of my decision, or that I had met all financial obligations to him. And I trusted Lemanczyk. He had been a pitcher in the major leagues for nearly ten years. As a former teammate, he knew me and understood the strained situation with my employers. He knew what I was going through because he had been in the same place.

Though our signatures were on documents that could make him my agent, they were signed on the understanding that any agreement was subject to confirmation. Like someone seeking a divorce, it would have been prudent of me to exercise great caution before proposing marriage again. As unhappy as I was with the result of Comte's efforts, I wanted to be extremely careful about whom I would entrust with such a sensitive area of my life.

To ensure my peace of mind, neither the original copy of the typewritten contract I took with me, nor the one Lemanczyk retained, were dated. This would be added only when, only if, I decided to let Lemanczyk act on my behalf. This was made abundantly clear and was a provision to which Lemanczyk agreed. If I wanted someone else to represent me, he would tear up the signed contracts. All I need do was tell him so.

That November, I phoned Lemanczyk and told him that I would not need his services. Lemanczyk sent me a letter stating he had stopped all activity on my behalf and, what's more, wished me good luck.

A little later, a mystified Pat Gillick telephoned me. He wanted to know whether Lemanczyk or Comte was my agent. Neither, I replied. The confusion had been caused when Lemanczyk sent the agent authorization forms to the players' association and to the club.

Soon, Comte was on the telephone to my home in Morgan Hill, California, suggesting we meet to discuss some vital matters. This turned out to be the threat of a lawsuit if I didn't sign a form confirming he was still my agent.

I signed, but if I needed further proof that Mr. Comte and Mr. Stieb were through, it was the threat of legal action.

It is said that important people come into your life at important times. If ever I needed a true friend, this was that time. Unknown to me, I had two working on my behalf.

One, a former schoolmate, got in touch with the other, my old football coach, and said he would be doing me a favor if he called me at this low point in my life. I was glad to hear from anyone who might be able to show me a way out of my difficulties.

The years had changed Bob Lamonte a great deal in some ways, only a little in others. He was still the big, gruff, no-bull sort of guy I had known when he taught history and coached Oak Grove High. He had majored in United States diplomatic history at Santa Clara University, minored in labor while working toward his doctorate at Stanford and had made a few bucks selling real estate.

Recently, he had become involved in a small way in representing players—among them Mervyn Fernandez of the Canadian Football League's B.C. Lions, Rich Campbell of the National Football League's Green Bay Packers, and some basketball and tennis players.

We talked a little on the telephone, the kind of stuff a coach and his former student might swap, and then I poured out my troubles. He volunteered, as a friend might do, that the last thing I needed was another agent complicating my life. What I needed, he said, was a competent lawyer.

The advice was simple. Do nothing, say nothing, sign nothing that had anything to do with either Comte or Lemanczyk until I was free of all contractual obligations early in February.

If there was a slight hitch, it was that Pat Gillick was making a swing through southern California early in February, at the time my contract with Comte would lapse, to talk with another player. For whatever reasons, there seemed to have been a warming in my relations with the club—a change, frankly, that I was eager to promote.

As might be imagined, I was weary of living from season to season with the uncertainty of one-year deals. My work indicated I was worthy of a contract that would secure the future. The club was on the verge of becoming a contender and wanted assurances of pitching strength in seasons to come.

The night the contract with Comte expired, Gillick happened to phone and said he and Paul Beeston, who controls the club's purse strings, would be in town the following day.

He hoped we could avoid resorting to arbitration to settle our differences. I shared his wish.

The hitch was that I had no one to talk for me and, in a delicate climate where an ill-timed remark might wreck any chance for peace, the last guy I wanted taking part in the negotiations was myself.

In desperation, I phoned Bob. He was up to his bifocals marking history papers, but he thought that he might be able to sound them out and, if their position offered any promise, lay the groundwork for whomever I might hire in the future. It told me a lot about Bob that, when I mentioned the subject of compensation, he said there was no need for a contract between us.

They began talks the next morning and, by midnight, Bob was on the phone with a progress report. Would I settle for six years and $7.5 million? I can't remember exactly what I said but it was something like, ''Yes!'' Even so, I had the feeling that things were going so well they just had to go bad.

I was right.

Here Comes the Judge

Signing my autograph cost me months of grief
and a cool $125,000 to settle the lawsuits

PICTURE, IF YOU WILL, a day at the beach.

Sun's high. Surf's up. The suds are in the cooler. Just to take the edge off the heat, it's time for a dip.

You're out there, floating, maybe a couple of hundred yards offshore—just you and the water and lots of sky. No sound, no cares, no reason to think there ever will be.

Now add a couple of fins, one on the left and one on the right.

I had discovered that money, like blood in salt water, draws sharks. There was plenty to tempt them.

That's how it was after Bob LaMonte, arranged a $6.6 million transfusion for my bank account.

The previous December, as is the custom with most front offices in the major leagues, the club mailed me an offer for my services during the 1983 season. After three years of failure to compromise with the club, including a fruitless attempt at arbitration the previous spring, there was no way I really expected anything to be substantially different this time around.

My thinking at the time was that I would have settled for something in the neighborhood of $500,000 that year. My bid, therefore, was for $750,000 and, since the club seemed to think I was worth nowhere near the lesser of these princely sums, I was intent on seeking the $750,000 in my second attempt at arbitration.

One need not be a career diplomat to figure out that the last thing an employer and employee need is the fallout from calling on a third party to settle a disagreement over money. Not only is one side upset that the other refuses to see reason in the first place, but the winner and loser leave the table all but assured of another squabble the next time the matter comes up for discussion.

Each side also presents the other with a risk neither really wants to face.

The player has no financial security beyond the current season. An off year, which he can be expected to blame on the club's refusal to be fair, undercuts his position when negotiations begin again the next winter. Worse, a career-ending injury deprives him of his big chance for security.

The club hastens the day when the blue-chip performer in whom they have invested a fortune in time and money leaps at the prospect of free agency.

Nobody wins. Everybody loses. Only a fool takes any pleasure in playing this kind of game and, let me assure you, fools have a way of playing or managing themselves out of this game. Quickly.

That's one of the reasons I dared to hope for success when Bob LaMonte agreed to present my case to club vice-presidents Pat Gillick (baseball) and Paul Beeston (finance) the day they stopped over in San Jose.

It eased my mind considerably that when I mentioned compensation to LaMonte the night before, he dismissed the subject as something that could be discussed later when, and if, I felt the need. In other words, he could have hammered out the $6.6 million contract he did that day and, without my signature to say any differently, I would not have had to part with a thin dime for all his efforts. It told me something and, just between us, it came as no surprise. The guy was more interested in my welfare than in making money for himself.

The morning the negotiations opened, I had hoped that I soon would be wearing a $750,000 smile. That LaMonte had exceeded my expectations by about $6 million, give or take a few grand, left me speechless for one of the few times in my life. When he said I could sign the following day, my first question was, "Why not tonight?"

My next question, as I piled into the Porsche and headed for the hotel, is one I have yet to answer. How could LaMonte, who had been representing me for all of fifteen minutes, negotiate security for a lifetime in one day when my former agent, Steve Comte, in my view, failed to get me one extra nickel in three years of trying?

For six years of service, including the bonus for signing, I would earn an average $1.1 million annually. If, in the impossible event that every one of my bonus clauses—Cy Young awards every year, make all the All-Star Games, win every ERA title—I could make a maximum $7.5 million. This, as you might well imagine, is called the "magic" part of the contract.

The club's policy is to guarantee no more than the first three years of any player's contract, a maximum that was granted to me. This meant my arm could fall off on the first delivery of opening day the following April and, no ifs, ands or buts about it, the Stieb family would receive $3.3 million over the next three seasons. Guarantees for the fourth, fifth and sixth years are activated by completing 225 innings the previous season. By meeting this condition last year, the last of the three in the original guarantee, I ensured my $1.1 million salary for this season.

Let us say, for the sake of a good argument, that I fell one inning short of the target. The club, by rights, could refuse to pay me my $1.1 million. We could either settle on a new figure or, by paying me $250,000 for each year remaining, they could buy their way out of the contract. Unless there had been an injury of a disabling nature or some catastrophic circumstance, I have to think it likely they would not quibble about $1.1 million. I would not, however, want to make a habit out of testing their good will.

This, I need hardly say, is a lot of money. Nor is a tenth of $7.5 million, which is what Dave Lemanczyk thought I owed him, what the working stiff would call peanuts.

I was under the impression that I had signed an agreement with Lemanczyk which was not binding and which I could cancel at any time. To show it was not binding, we didn't date it. I called Lemanczyk a few months after signing this document to cancel our agreement. He wrote to me, acknowledging the cancellation, and even wished me good luck. As far as I was concerned, Lemanczyk had never acted on my behalf. Three months later, Bob LaMonte negotiated (on my behalf) an excellent deal with the club. Wonder of wonders, Lemanczyk turned up and demanded an agent's cut, $750,000 to be exact, of my earnings.

Much as I dreaded putting my fate in any but my own hands, I told him we would be glad to thrash it out in court. I admit I was worried.

Pat Gillick, the man I once had perceived as my economic antagonist, did much in a personal and professional way to ease my fears. In addition to spending several days in New York, at the club's expense, helping us prepare our case, his testimony before Judge Thomas P. Greisa, United States District Court, Southern District of New York, did much to prove our point.

It was Gillick's fabled capacity for recall, in fact, that provided what my counsel considered one of our most telling arguments. He remembered that, at the time Lemanczyk approached me in New York, he was under contract as a scout for the Yankee organization. This suggested, strongly, a conflict of interest—a situation we stressed in cross-examination.

Another important point was the date (June 9, 1982). Lemanczyk's copy of the provisional agreement was dated. Mine was not. He testified that I signed it the day of a night game in which I played. Since I could prove I did not pitch that particular night, we argued that it showed the document had been back-dated.

We also suggested Lemanczyk was remiss in performing the duties of an agent by not ensuring that I was insured against a career-threatening injury. One would think, we argued, that an agent would remedy such a situation, particularly in view of my potential earnings and, subsequently, as an obvious source of income for an agent.

In his ruling the next day, Judge Greisa emphasized that he believed my version of why the contract was not dated. Also instrumental to our case was Lemanczyk's "goodbye" letter.

The relief could not have been greater had Tom Henke sailed in from the bullpen and whiffed Lemanczyk on three pitches with the bases loaded and two out in the ninth inning.

Winning the suit made my position that much stronger when Comte and I appeared before the arbitrator in California. He ordered me to pay him $3,500. This was compensation for the month of "services" that followed signing the agreement that confirmed him as my agent after Lemanczyk sent papers to the club and the players' union.

It bothered me to part with money for nothing but, considering my happiness over being rid of these encumbrances, it was worth the price. Still, when I think that it cost me $125,000 in legal fees and expenses to be free, I have to say it makes me nervous every time I pick up a pen.

Now that I was happy, now that all my grievances had

been put to rest, I set about doing all that I could to see that the team and its fans got full value for their money. Business is business and, since it had been done to my satisfaction, baseball was going to be a pleasure again.

So the money was right. An important point, to be sure, but just as surely, not the only one worth considering. Beneath the acrimony that marked my first three years with the organization was the very real fear that I would not be around when this promising team started making good.

As deep as my American roots go, as much as I love the country of my birth, it would have broken my heart to spend my summers anywhere but Toronto. As cities go, it is big enough to draw 2.5 million fans a season, yet it retains the best elements of a town you might find on any rural route in the United States. It is polite. It is clean. It is safe. Yes, it is much easier to tell spring from summer than it might be in Oakland or Arlington, but the weather is no worse than it can be in Detroit, New York or Boston. The fans might be on the quiet side—less so since they started selling beer at the park a couple of years back—but they come out in droves and they're nothing like the inmates of some zoos we have had the misfortune to visit in recent years.

I am reasonably certain I could have opted for free agency sometime in the future, at a time when my abilities remained near their peak. There is no telling what might have been, but if Bruce Sutter, as fine a reliever as he can be, commands $48 million from the Atlanta Braves, I had to think I could have cashed my chips somewhere in the same vicinity. Believe it or not, there comes a point with me when enough is enough. What could I do with $50 million that I couldn't do with half as much?

There is no need for me to name the names of owners, or cities in which their teams play, that could not buy my services for all the gold in Fort Knox. People might scoff when I say there is no place I would rather play out my career, but the proof is in the fact that just before the '85 season got under way, I signed what amounts to a lifetime contract.

It is something I cannot see myself ever regretting.

I was most attentive when, toward the end of the '84 season, the club suggested we discuss arrangements that would link our destinies for the remainder of my playing days. Since the management is squarely against renegotiating contracts, a policy players accept so long as there are no exceptions, we had to find a way of circumventing the fact that my first agreement had four more years to run at the time. In other words, as agent Bob LaMonte pointed out when we discussed the situation, we had to make "something out of nothing."

We settled on a seven-year extension of that contract, in effect committing me to another eleven seasons with the club starting in 1984.

The money? Oh, yes, the money.

It amounts to $25 million, including an annuity of $10 million payable in twenty installments of $500,000 that start following my last year of service. In addition, there are incentives to a maximum of $8 million, about $4 million of which I consider to be within reach.

In the first year of the extension, my salary rises from about $1 million to $1.6 million. It increases $100,000 annually until it reaches $2.2 million in the final year. The first two years are guaranteed if I pitch 225 innings the previous season. Thereafter, as I get older, the figure drops to 212 each year.

The enticement of an annuity—a carrot no longer offered by major league clubs—is that it allows the athlete to delay paying substantial amounts of tax dollars during peak earnings. Later, when his income declines, the bite on the dollars he has squirrelled away is far less severe.

The real beauty of this annuity, to pick up the "something for nothing" theme, is that I paid my $400,000 share of it with some of the bonus money I received for signing the extension. Over the life of the total contract, the club pays $5 to my $1. What this means, basically, is that we pay about $1.6 million for a $10 million return.

When the annuity lapses, about the time I turn fifty-seven, payments from the players' union pension plan begin. Five years later, at age sixty-two, my tax dollars begin to trickle back in the form of a government pension.

I will take it, of course, but it is my most ardent hope that I will not be in need of it.

Champs

When champagne bubbles in the dressing room
the rule is, "Wear it well, but never, ever drink it"

CHAMPAGNE, CHAMPAGNE EVERYWHERE, but not a drop
worth drinking.

One would think the club would have splurged for the
best brand of bubbly there is, knowing that after almost ten
years of sweat, toil and pulled hamstrings in the American
League, its first division championship was in the bag.

But n-o-o-o, not a fifty-dollar bottle of Dom Perignon
was in evidence that Saturday afternoon last October when
Doyle Alexander, who had just cooled the New York Yankees 5–1 on five hits, was carted by his admiring teammates
back into the madhouse that, a few short hours before, had
been a dressing room as quiet as a church at eventide.

It soon became clear, however, that the bosses, in their
infinite wisdom, had been right to keep a close eye on the
folding stuff when they opted for vinegar ordinaire to conse-
crate this victory so long in the making. When the stuff is in
your hair, pouring out your ears, running down your back,
sloshing around in your sweat socks, I defy any connoisseur

to tell me the difference between Dommy P '59 and Sneaky Pete '85 strained through a pair of Jim Acker's longjohns.

It was not a matter of taste, as one might have surmised from Alexander's reaction when George Bell, who made the final out, bear-hugged the man of the hour and thrust a foaming flagon towards him. "Don't drink the stuff," he drawled, holding fast to the bottle of beer he had just fished out of the clubhouse cooler. Worlds apart where pitching philosophies are concerned, I have to admit that in this matter of personal preference, we are unanimous. Not only does champagne make my ears roar, my eyes go runny and my nose crinkle up, but I tend to guzzle the stuff like cream soda. This, experience has taught me, makes the room spin when I lie down on the rug and pretend to count the little holes in the ceiling.

Except for the clubhouse crew (Ian Duff, Kevin Malloy, Greg Kimoff, Paul Gillis) who generally will drink anything so long as it is wet, very little of this stuff was being used for the purpose of quaffing toasts to the ecstasy of victory. Their boss, Jeff Ross, whose tastes are a little more refined, had wisely seen to it that his henchmen had wreathed the lockers in plastic sheeting. Good thing, too. Within minutes, floors, walls, rafters and anybody in the vicinity were sopping wet with champagne.

It is said that to become a major leaguer, the dream of every little boy, means never having to grow up. Though there are many times during the season when I would dispute this notion, I now tend to agree with it after having taken part in the three-ring circus that pitched its tent in our clubhouse that Saturday afternoon. As unseemly as it might appear to those who consider themselves capable of maintaining a sense of decorum when all about them are losing theirs, I must say that jiggling a bottle of bubbly and nailing anything that moves with a geyser of goo is more fun than tipping an outhouse, preferably occupied, on Hallowe'en.

Childish? Maybe. But, gee whiz, mom, I'm only twenty-eight.

Once the first tidal wave had subsided, leaving a mist of sweet bubbly in its wake, I settled back in the chair by my locker and began soaking up the sea of faces swirling around me. This was something that I wanted to remember for a long time and, if I was to do it, I would have to pay a little attention.

At one point, a thought entered my mind, one that occurs to each of us in the final days of any season: who wouldn't be there the following spring when we opened camp next spring in Dunedin? The year before, Jim Gott, Dave Collins and Alfredo Griffin left this clubhouse for the last time. Who would be the first to go this time?

Pat Gillick, the architect of the club, had said the club would not be active in the pursuit of free agents, but expected a turnover of twenty per cent just the same. Infielder Manny Lee and outfielder Lou Thornton, fine prospects we were forced to keep on the roster for the season or send back to the clubs that had lost them in the draft, surely would return to the minors to continue their apprenticeships. Would there be a place for Al Oliver and Jeff Burroughs? Would Rick Leach, a pal from the days of Alaska, come north with us next spring? Would Buck Martinez, injured in a crash at home plate in Seattle, come back after breaking a leg and dislocating an ankle? And always there was the spectre of a trade, like the ones that brought us Gary Lavelle and Bill Caudill last winter, that might take other faces from our midst.

My thoughts were interrupted by the commotion in the middle of the room as Bobby Cox, the manager who had taken us from the outhouse to the penthouse, made his entrance after a shower in the coaches' quarters up the hallway.

Had someone suggested to me that he would be the first to go, I would have staked my World Series share (bad joke) against a broken bat quicker than an umpire calls ball four.

Like every other baseball fan in the free world, we had heard talk that Ted Turner wanted him back in Atlanta as GM and field manager of the Braves. And, like everyone, we kissed it off when Chuck Tanner got the field job. None of us figured Coxie for a suit, tie and desk job. Even after a winter to adjust, it was strange not to see him propping up the batting cage at spring camp this year.

Sure, I'm expected to say as much, but I honestly can't think of a better guy to replace him than Jimy Williams. He was long overdue for a manager's job and, from what I hear, was next-to-last cut a number of times when the position was filled on other teams. Not only is he familiar with the team, after six seasons as second-in-command to Coxie and Bobby Mattick before him, but he possesses one of the finest tactical minds in the game today. Easy to get along with if you do your work, but no pushover in the discipline department, the transition could not have been smoother under anyone else.

If I have any regrets—forgive me if I show a little sentiment here—it has to be that I never got around to telling Coxie how much I thought of him while he was here. Come to think of it, there are a couple of stories from his playing days that lead me to believe we had more than a little in common.

By way of setting up the first one, let me say that I go through two or three fielder's gloves a season. I prefer them to be a little on the stiff side, so the moment the one I use for games starts losing its elasticity, I begin the process of breaking in the next one during practice. Other guys become so attached to them that, rather than be parted, they would scrap the no-trade-to-Cleveland clause in their multi-year contracts.

When Coxie got his $40,000 to sign with the Los Angeles Dodgers in 1959, the story goes, he went out and spent twenty-five dollars of it on a four-fingered Wilson model glove. I have no idea what became of the remaining $39,975, nor is it any of my business, but he still has the glove that followed him to such exotic outposts as Reno, Panama City, Albuquerque, Salt Lake City, Tacoma, Austin, Richmond and, for two seasons with the Yankees, New York. He kept it to pitch batting practice when he managed in Fort Lauderdale, West Haven, Syracuse, Atlanta and Toronto. By the end of the '84 season, after nearly a quarter of a century of service, it was in such a state that, had it been Old Shep, the right thing to do would have been to take it out behind the barn and put it out of its misery. Anybody but Coxie might have. Instead, a shoemaker pal of his took it in over the winter and, after a series of leather transplants and more stitches than they sew in a month at Toronto General, it made a miraculous return to life. The way Coxie would go on about this guy who saved his beloved glove, you'd think he was a twenty-game winner. About the only other time it left his side, so the story goes, was the day in the minors that a teammate figured it would be a nifty joke to swipe it. Coxie got it back after he put his fist through a window of the team bus.

It's a good thing, now that I think about it, that a couple of the fellows on our club never did carry out their plan to swipe that glove and have it stuffed, mounted and bronzed as a token of the high esteem in which they held him.

The other story also involves his playing days. Coxie, whose knees are in the same shape as his old glove used to be, belongs to that school of players who have endured pain so long that they might not feel healthy without it. His days as a player were over before he was thirty, which must have broken his heart, even if the blow was softened somewhat with the start of his managerial career with Fort Lauderdale in the Florida State League. Anyway . . . it seems that Coxie wrecked his right shoulder toward the end of one season and, all that following winter, he practised throwing with his left arm, hoping he might be able to make the conversion from third to first base. Coxie, when he tells this story, laughs from his heels when he admits this masterful plan eventually strained the left shoulder worse than the right one.

I'm all for a guy who takes himself seriously in this business, but he's missing a lot of what life is all about when he can't laugh at the practical jokes it sends his way. It is an element, I must admit, that could stand a little development in me.

In their own curious way, now that I look back on them, these two stories underline the qualities of loyalty and spirit that are foremost in the man. Still, though these may be the traits that earn a place in heaven, they are not worth a nickel on a ticket to the Hall of Fame unless they are coupled with ability, brains and the courage to apply them. As much as he will say he had the players, it was no coincidence that in his four seasons with us the club advanced from nowhere (78–84) to the top of the heap (99–62). It also proves that nice guys don't always finish last.

Back to the party.

Across the way, somewhere behind the banks of lights and the jerry-rigged podium that has become a target range for champagne marksmen, is Ernie Whitt, whose second-inning home run on a 3–2 pitch from Joe Cowley was the spark that lit the fuse to the dynamite. One of the three Jays remaining from that first camp in 1977, the catcher manager Roy Hartsfield voted least likely to succeed, he proved there is room in this game for those whose talent needs only a chance to overhaul their work ethic.

It was also a day of reclamation for center fielder Lloyd Moseby who, only the evening before, had cost us the game when a routine fly popped out of his glove to allow the winning run in the top of the ninth. If ever there was a case to be made for my contention that baseball does not build character as much at it reveals it, then Moseby has to be Exhibit

Number One. Others might have been destroyed by this dreadful turn of luck, but he responded with a home run in the third on another 3–2 pitch by Cowley. His great and good friend, Willie Upshaw, who seems to travel in lockstep, followed with another smash. This game, this division title, was in the history books. It was something no one could ever take from us.

There were others, too, who did their bit to bring us to the threshold of this magnificent day.

Finally, after waiting four seasons, Jesse Barfield proved he could play every day (and then some) with twenty-seven home runs and twenty-two assists to lead the league.

Of the twenty-eight home runs George Bell smacked to lead the club, three of them were the longest I have ever seen and, incredibly, were hit on consecutive days at Comiskey Park in Chicago. Between driving each one over the roof in right field and left field, Tom Seaver managed to keep him in the park with a 455-foot rocket into the seats behind center field.

Rance Mulliniks and Garth Iorg make up the best two-headed third baseman in the game, a switch-hitter with a .300 average, seventeen home runs and a fielding average of .970.

In only his second season, Tony Fernandez drew raves with his glove and surprised a lot of people with a .289 batting average. Damaso Garcia, always hurt, got in his 600 at-bats and drove home sixty-five runs from the leadoff position.

And the pitchers.

Alexander and Acker, Clancy and Caudill, Key and Lamp, Lavelle and Henke, Filer and Musselman and whoever else won that one crucial game somewhere along the way that put us into the playoffs for the first time.

The coaches, too. Uncle Al (The Pitcher's Pal) Widmar and Jimy Williams. Cito Gaston and John Sullivan and Billy the (57-year-ol') Kid Smith. And the trainers, who could forget the trainers? Ken Whatshisname and Tommy Who. OK, OK, Carson and Craig.

Not for the first time has this been said, nor I daresay for the last, but it will serve as the appropriate epitaph for what went into that fine afternoon.

It was a team effort.

Older than Springtime

When it's my time to leave the game for good,
they'll have to drag me screaming and kicking

SPRINGTIME IS SUPPOSED TO BE a time for new beginnings, but I have yet to see a March become an April before some old pro had to be told he wouldn't be going north with the club this time.

It's sad. Really sad.

You wonder why he didn't see it coming; why he didn't get out with his dignity intact; why he didn't listen when his eyes or his arms or his legs were telling him they could give no more.

Later that night, maybe an hour after the lights have been snuffed and my wife is fast asleep, I'll be at the kitchen table staring at a couple of cookies and a glass of milk.

As much as I hate to admit it, if they can tell Rod Carew his services no longer are required, I know that one day they will have to tell me to take a hike. No way will I go quietly. How, I will kid myself, do you know you're through? How can you sit down that awful day and say, I know I'm done, when, all those other days all those other years, you talked

yourself into believing you still had it? There have to be a
few more pitches left on the old arm, a few more games, one
last season. I'll pitch as long as somebody wants me and, if
they don't, I'll go somewhere else until there is nowhere else
to go.

It would be a lot easier for all concerned, I think, if the
parting came at the end of a season instead of at the beginning. Spend seven months with twenty-four guys—in spring
training, then in another country, then in all those hotels on
the road—and getting away from it all becomes a little more
attractive as propositions go. Maybe if you had a few months
to get used to the idea, without the boxscores to remind you
every morning, it would be a lot easier to handle.

And then again, maybe not.

Spring training, where winning or losing is not equated
with life and death, is one of the best parts of the season.
Wind, rain, slush and snow tires . . . with any luck, they'll
be history by Opening Day back in Toronto.

If there's a hitch, and there are always a couple, it is that
not all of the faces you saw in the clubhouse that night last
October came to Dunedin this spring.

No more Bobby Cox.

As much as we all were relieved and approved of Jimy
Williams getting the manager's job, somehow I had a hard
time getting it through my head that I would never see Coxie,
hands stuffed in his jacket pockets, make that long, gimpy-
legged trip to the mound.

Where's Al Oliver? Jeff Burroughs? Where's Ron Musselman? Lou Thornton and Manny Lee will be back, I know,
but at the cost of someone else's departure.

This year, for a while anyway, injuries relieved (if that's
the word) Jimy Williams of the responsibility of having to
make substantial cuts. Tom Filer, his elbow a mess, was out
for the season after an operation. Gary Lavelle also had to

wonder if his days were numbered after he underwent arm surgery. Bill Caudill felt a tug in his right shoulder making a pitch during spring training. He started the season on the disabled list and was used only sparingly over the next couple of months.

The year before it was good pal Jim Gott, the spirited Alfredo Griffin and the game Dave Collins. The compensation is that they went to steady jobs. With the younger, gifted Tony Fernandez capable of hitting .300, the day was hastening when Griffin would sit on the bench. With George Bell, Lloyd Moseby and Jesse Barfield in the outfield, Collins's days also were numbered. What Gott needed, win or lose, was a job where he got the ball every fourth day.

The trades set up a chain reaction known by the baseball fraternity as the numbers game. It can produce a sudden chill on what are supposed to be the sunniest days of the season.

Caudill and Lavelle, obtained at the cost of Griffin, Collins and Gott, gave us the right-left relief combination in the late innings. Add the five starters and that left three spots on a ten-man pitching staff. Make that two if you bought the theory that, with seven scheduled days off in April, Jimmy Key could alternate as long reliever and starter. Heads would roll and, give or take Jim Clancy's inflamed appendix, the only question was how many.

Roy Lee Jackson and Bryan Clark drew the short straws and, worse for them, it happened late in spring training when most rosters were set. Jackson, devoutly religious, must have had his faith put to the test. Had he made the team, his one-year contract called for about $400,000. The Orioles signed him to a Triple A contract and sent him to Rochester, New York, where he would make about $25,000. He made it back to the majors, with the San Diego Padres, and landed in Minneapolis early in the '86 season when the Minnesota Twins got off to a rough start. Clark, after a stint in the minors, wound up in Cleveland, but was cut at the end of the season. He, too, got another life with the Chicago White Sox and, in fact, pitched well against us in a game in May '86.

It happens every spring at every camp, an immutable law of nature wherever baseball is played, but a thing, nonetheless, to which you never become inured. What you tell a guy is that he is not good enough to be here. Any way you put the sugar on it, it is humiliating.

And what do the other players tell the guy?

If you say nothing, it is as if you agree with the assessment. This is no knock on management. It has to be the worst part of the manager's job, maybe as bad as getting canned himself, but the players share a natural affinity with each other. Cut him, in other words, and it has to take a nick out of me. Somehow, you convey that you care, really care; that what he is or is not between the lines has no bearing on what he means to you. You tell him, "Good luck. Hope to see you around." It sounds so lame, even if you do mean it. I wish them well, against everybody but us.

Apart from the letting of blood and the fact that, for everyone except the sports writers, it is two weeks too long, spring training is among the best of times a ball player can have.

After a four-month furlough, no matter how much I like home cooking and playing make-believe Jack Nicklaus, the craving to play baseball, to be one of the boys again, is strong. I like to think it's like the first week of school. The heavy homework, the exams, all that is later. Right now, it's recess time. Easy does it. Don't run when you can walk. Don't walk when you can sit. Don't sit when you can find a cool spot in the outfield to flake out. And just about the time you're ready, just when the juices get flowing, the games begin.

I agree that winning or losing here is not as serious as it becomes in April, but I've never been able to persuade myself to feel as good after a loss as I do after winning. I think, too, that even if the Grapefruit League Champ is rarely there when the Fall Classic is decided, I'd sooner win it than lose it.

One of the best things about it, at least on days when we play teams from the National League, is that I get to prove again to Ernie (Bigfoot) Whitt how well I can hit.

I think it was in St. Pete against the Cards a couple of years back that I provided my last demonstration of the dynamics involved in the launching of an air-to-ground missile. Bigfoot was on second base with a double and, abiding by the cardinal rule of baseball when a pitcher is ahead 2–0 in the count, Jimy Williams flashed several take signs from his coach's box at third base. Maybe it says something for my powers of concentration, but I saw nothing.

Fastball, right down the pipe. I hit it so squarely that it darted two or three times before it kicked up a divot in front of the left fielder. Whitt, who had seen Williams's signs, was caught off guard and started late for home. As he chugged around third, the outfielder picked up the ball and launched his throw to the plate. Slowpoke was out by only ten or fifteen feet, robbing me of what would have been, should have been, my first RBI in the major leagues.

It was worth it, considering the howl he put up in the clubhouse.

On and on he went. How a real hitter can read a coach's signs, even if they aren't as simple as the one, two or three fingers the catcher flashes when I'm on the mound. How one half of the pensioners in the stands that day could hit a ball that far and the other half even farther. How the swiftest mutt from the dog track nearby couldn't have beat that lucky stiff's throw home.

We all knew, of course, that Ernie, a little thin on top, was afraid he'd run out from under his cap.

Which reminds me . . .

Though I make my money *pitching* a baseball and though my contributions as a professional to the art of hitting are minimal—19-for-99 (.192) as a part-time outfielder for Dunedin of the Florida State League in 1978—and even though I risk more abuse from the aforementioned Mr. Whitt, I have a few worthwhile theories on the art of hitting.

To say they are the fruit of my own fertile imagination would make me a liar. They came to me by way of John Oldham, a crusty old southpaw said to have had a flame of a temper in his time, who managed the team at San Jose City College. My brother Steve, who had won the catching job there the year before, swore by Oldham and, because of his strong recommendation, I turned down a four-year scholarship at the state university. Smart move, too.

The bag of tricks the oldtimer laid before us—which involved hours of theory at the blackboard, one of the rare times I have been fascinated by what went on in a classroom—ranged from the commonsense to the sublime.

In the first category was his belief that the sooner a hitter started tracking a pitched ball, the more likely he was to hit it. Therefore, we fixed our eyes at the spot beside the pitcher's head where the ball, making its arc in the pitcher's hand, would first appear. Coach Oldham took it a step further, defining three areas of impact on the ball: 1) top, which would produce a grounder; 2) center, which would produce a line drive; 3) bottom, which would produce a pop-up. Choose Number 2, of course, and you go to the head of the class. What this focusing process also accomplishes is quicker recognition of the type of spin being imparted on the ball by the pitcher and, therefore, the clue to where it will be when it approaches the plate.

At the other end of the scale was a process he termed successful visualization. It appealed to me right away because the first step involved lying down and thinking cool thoughts. Waves lapping at a sun-stroked beach in California. Dusk casting its tall shadows across the Mojave Desert. The snow-capped peaks of the San Bernardino Mountains. That sort of thing. At the moment you felt calmest, you coined a key word. Beach. Desert. Mountains. That sort of thing.

Right about now, if I can read your mind, you're wondering what languid thoughts have to do with beating the bejammers out of a baseball.

A lot.

The first rule of hitting, among the most difficult to heed when a batter settles in the box to face a series of 90 m.p.h. pitches, is to be relaxed. Since it is considered bad form to lie down, at least until the first pitch is on its way, the best a hitter can do is put his mind at ease. Say the key word that reminds you of the state of calm and how it was achieved. Next, look to the side of the pitcher's head for the release point of the ball. Picture in your mind the ball heading toward the plate. Imagine the Number 2 spot as it leaves his hand. See it float to the plate and watch it find the gap between the outfielders. Successful visualization—or, if you prefer, the self-fulfilling prophecy as it applies to baseball.

Another fun part of spring training is that you get a chance to see how you rate against some of the game's greats in the other league. The only other opportunity, if you're lucky enough or good enough, comes during the All-Star Game (three innings at the most) or in the World Series (four games, preferably). That's why I wouldn't mind a season schedule that included play with the National League.

If not for spring training and all-star games, I never would have had the pleasure of facing Pete Rose, a legend in anybody's book, including this one. I wish I could rave on about the battles we've had, but the truth is our confrontations were not the stuff of which *War and Peace* was made.

Facing Charlie Hustle, hell-bent on surpassing Ty Cobb's 4,191 hits at the time, is in the same category for me as staring down the barrel of Reggie Jackson's bat. You know you are in the company of the best who ever played this game. You like to think some of it will rub off on you.

The problem is that, as hitters go, Rose is as impatient as a bull in the breeder's shed. He would always jump on the first couple of pitches and, hit or out, he would be out of my clutches. It would give me precious little to tell the grandchildren about when, after climbing upon my arthritic knee, they asked what I did during the twenty-five-year war Pete Rose waged on an army of pitchers.

They just might have to settle with what follows and, like a fifty-five-foot fastball, it is not very much.

This particular afternoon, he had taken his customary two swings on his first couple of trips to the plate and, if memory serves, I think he grounded out both times. Third time up, I tell myself, we'll battle. Half a dozen pitches, maybe a few fouls, then whiff, he's gone. I wanted it. Badly.

He whacked the first pitch into center field for a single. Dammit. I watched him, pleased as punch, his foot on first base, that kid's grin on his face just like he'd squashed a bug. I threw up my hands.

"I got thousands of those," he says to me. Geez, one of my heroes, and now he thinks I begrudge him one little hit. Next time up, though, he hit into a double play. As he trots back to the dugout, I admit I'm thinking of telling him I've had hundreds of those.

I guess I'm just too nice a guy.

Hurtin'

*Big Jim and Buck had it far, far worse than me
but the ache in my arm is a pain in the neck*

IT BEGAN HURTING IN MARCH OF '85 and, like the poor relation who refuses to see that the doorbell is busted and the welcome mat has been yanked, it was still hurting in March of '86.

For such a little muscle in the forearm — one of a group of flexors that join near the elbow, Doc Taylor told me that day at Grant Field in Dunedin— it has caused me one huge pain in the, ahem, vicinity of my hip pocket.

The flexors, as the throbbing reminded me, are located on the sunny side of the forearm. To feel them work, put the first two fingers of the left hand just below the joint of the right elbow, ball up the fist and rotate the wrist. Then think about the mayhem that little bit of gristle goes through in the course of a baseball season. At 35 starts, maybe 125 pitches per, that's nearly 4,500 times that I put it to its maximum test. And that's not counting the fifteen to eighteen minutes of warming up each time out, the throwing on the side between starts or tossing the ball around the outfield during batting practice. It was no big surprise, therefore, when the flexors led the jeering section on mornings after I had done my tour on the mound.

Don't get me wrong. I'm not saying the '85 and '86 seasons were one long bed of hot coals through which I was forced to tread in my sweatsocks. If I were looking for a case of hard luck, I'd go no further than ten feet to the locker where Jim Clancy spent a large chunk of the '85 season. He looked the picture of good health that spring and, just listening to the pop his pitches made when they hit the mitt, we figured him for the best season of his career. Then appendicitis knocks him out of the box and it's months before he can put it together again. Just when he's right and wins five in a row, his shoulder gives out. Tendinitis. Not so bad, considering that he first thought it was a tear in the rotator cuff—which, by any other name, is the kiss of death for a pitcher. And never a whisper from him, either, but that's Clancy. He could lose a perfect game in the ninth on a bloop single, as he once did, and he might shrug his shoulders.

And Buck Martinez. His leg was broken and his ankle dislocated on a play at the plate in Seattle and, while he was flirting with insensibility, he tossed the ball into left field trying to get Gorman Thomas running to third. George Bell fielded it, winged it back to the plate and Martinez tagged out Thomas. Weirdest double play I ever saw. The most costly, too.

It might be true, as the saying goes, that they also serve who only stand and wait, but you cannot persuade an injured player this is so. We did all we could to make Clancy and Martinez feel they were part of the team, but they knew they couldn't do their bit on the field. There is no pain that cuts deeper than the feeling, right or wrong, of not being able to contribute.

While we are on the subject of courage, let me air one of my pet peeves: people who suggest this is a game for gentlemen athletes. The way they talk, you'd think we took tea breaks every three innings.

Ask Damaso Garcia or Tony Fernandez what a luxury resort second base can be when a runner throws a body block on the front end of a double play. Nobody ever promised Lloyd Moseby a rose garden when he came to the major leagues, but he would be a happier man by far without the raspberry patch he gathered on his, well, hide while swiping fifty-six bases last season. And when George Brett and his bat, all of sixty feet, six inches away, swat your best fastball back where it came from, you discover the difference between being quick and being dead is a fine line indeed.

There was a time when I thought, as all those who have never been wounded are likely to do, that I was immortal. Ernest Riles, a rookie infielder with the Milwaukee Brewers, shattered my sense of invulnerability one summer day in '85 when he lined a ball off my right leg a couple of inches above the knee. I felt it, but what really frightens me is that I never saw it. A couple of inches lower, a few inches higher (ouch) and I would not have escaped with a case of minor swelling.

The injury that ends a career, the one that is waiting to happen the next time you pick up a ball and send it on its way, is a fact of life with which the professional must learn to live. In my case, what makes it a little easier is the long-term contract that guarantees I will get a lot of money in the event that, on some black day, they have to carry me off on my shield. What would hurt worse, the injury without a scar, would be knowing I would never play this game again. I cannot think of life without baseball.

Everyone wants the Purple Heart, I suppose, but nobody wants to be wounded. Then again, if you pitch, the axiom is that you learn to pitch with pain.

A cross between a minor toothache and a severe bruise,

my flexors nagged me through most of '85 although, for some curious reason, the difficulty vanished for about ten starts in the middle of the season. At the best of times, I was aware of it. At the worst of times, it got in the way.

If it was going to happen again this spring, I assured myself it wouldn't be for lack of effort to prevent it. After a month of digesting the season and airing out my thoughts, I started on a weight program. Nothing strenuous, mind you, like bench presses, curls and the like. The one thing a ballplayer doesn't need is bulk. Remember the horrendous season (14 homers, 49 RBI, .194 average) Reggie Jackson had in '83? He blamed it on a weight-training program that made him musclebound. What he didn't take into account is that most people lift weights to develop muscles like he already had. He adapted, which is the hallmark of great hitters, and last year at the age of thirty-nine, he proved he could still hit twenty-five to thirty homers a season. The way he came out of the gate this season suggests, too, that life does indeed begin at forty.

My goal was to strengthen the muscles I use in pitching, which entails a lot of light weights. I also started running in January and, since a few more of our players moved to Dunedin last winter, I had people to play catch with me. Again, nothing intense, just a little soft tossing on the back lawn or at the park beginning late in January.

What is it they say about the best-laid plans of mice and men? In my last outing of spring training, as I sat in the dugout between innings, that little spot near my elbow commanded my attention.

I have never gotten off to a poorer start than I did this season but, to be honest, my mechanics were mainly at fault.

To ease the long-term strain on my arm, I decided to add a hard curve to my arsenal. It would break much the same way as the slider. With my arm coming up too high, pitching coach Al Widmar pointed out late in April, I lost the precision on my release point and stopped following through. Trying to correct the habit, while working against major-league hitters, was not easy.

What might have contributed to the injury last season was an occasional tendency to land on a stiffened left leg, rather than bending it as I follow through in my delivery. The sudden stop triggered a recoil on the upper body and, as a result, there was a whiplash effect on the forearm.

Maybe I should have missed a start or two somewhere, but I would have hated to miss the assignments and still have the ailment when I came back.

In all honesty, I can't say that it affected either the velocity or the quality of pitches I made last season. Once I was warm, which took about five minutes more than usual, there would be no pain until late in the game. If there is a factor that tended to make it worse, it was having to wait in the dugout through a long inning. There is no way a pitcher, even those not in their right minds, will encourage his team to get fewer walks, hits and runs. When it comes to choosing between a little tightness in the elbow and a couple of crooked numbers on the scoreboard, there is no choice.

What's happening, I guess, is that I am getting older and the wear of 1,600 innings in the majors is not something to be dismissed as lightly as it might have been when I was a kid of twenty-two.

What made my cross harder to bear is that dealing with injury is a relatively uncommon experience for me. Prior to the difficulties with my forearm, my most pressing ailment was a blister that dogged me through the '83 and '84 seasons.

In comparison with what Martinez, Clancy, et al. suffered, my complaints are about as feeble as the swinging bunt. Just the same, isn't it the insignificant—the dripping faucet, the mysterious rattle in the family jalopy, the squeaking hinge—that drives a body to distraction?

The blister surfaced, and that's the word for it, on a muggy day in Chicago midway through the '83 season and, in part, was the result of an obsession I had developed for the slider. To throw this pitch, which breaks sharply to my left and down as it approaches the plate, requires putting pressure on the seam of the ball with the middle finger and, as it is released, snapping the wrist to exagerrate the spin off that finger.

Anyone who works with their hands has had a blister. Put a bandage on it, give it time to heal, muddle along for a few days. No problem. The hitch, in my profession, is that I am forced to aggravate it every fourth or fifth day. Had I been allowed to cover it, as any workman would be, it would have healed much more quickly, but the rules of baseball do not allow the pitcher to use "foreign substances" that might come in contact with the ball. That would put the poor, mis-begotten, benighted batter at a disadvantage. This rule applies, mind you, only if the perpetrator is caught doing it.

Flesh-colored as it was, no one seemed to notice the bandage wrapped around the tip of my middle finger. I swear on my 1986 copy of the *Official Baseball Register* that I put it on before doing the breakfast dishes and forgot to remove it when I left for the park.

Amos Otis, his reflexes dimmed after fourteen seasons in the Kansas City outfield, was parked on the bench that day. At thirty-six years of age, however, there was little wrong with his eyesight. Of course, he blew the whistle on me. I knew I was in trouble as soon as plate umpire John Shulock took off his mask and started the slow walk to the mound. Dammit, the sticky stuff was so good that it resisted all my fumbling attempts to peel it off and find a hiding place for the evidence.

Busted. Red-handed, so to speak. It could have been worse, I guess. I professed ignorance, mounted my best imper-sonation of the honest-if-flawed human being and pleaded for another chance. He rolled his eyes, in that "What will they think of next?'' way that umpires have, and told me to undress the dressing and get back to the game. The way the Royals were splitting their sides laughing, you had to think they were in need of a bandage or two.

If there was a blessing over my next dozen or so starts that year, it was that I learned to rely more on the fastball, an eminently acceptable pitch and a little easier to control, that brought me to the major leagues. Less reliance on the slider the next two seasons kept my blister problems to a minimum in '84 and eliminated it last year. I hear, too, that a thin film of pine tar mixed with resin not only works wonders on sensitive skin, but also improves the break on the slider. Nothing I would ever do, mind you, but the hitters would never take my word for it.

An injury more threatening, yet with the sense of the ridiculous that seems to track me, was the ankle I sprained six weeks before the '84 season. It was the same one I broke in '72 sliding into third base during my sophomore year in high school. While I was on crutches, I put so much pressure on the other ankle that it, too, suffered. For the whole of the season, I had to have both ankles taped prior to every game.

I guess I should be thankful that, entering the season, I had yet to spend my first day on the disabled list. In this regard, I have to agree with the philosophy that luck is the residue of design. One of the factors contributing to my durability is that, save for some spot duty and some work at the batting cage in my college days, I didn't become a pitcher until I signed a pro contract. As kids, there was no way my parents would let either Steve or me pitch. If my dad had an idea I'd make it one day to the majors, he was one up on me, but I have to believe this decision he made on my behalf was a major factor.

How much wear on my arm it saved may not be clear until my career is at an end. Nolan Ryan, who turns forty next January, still throws a fastball at ninety-plus m.p.h. and they say he clocked in the low eighties the first time he tossed his baby rattle. I would presume too much, therefore, if I said someone should or should not take up pitching until later in life, when the body is strong enough to take the strain.

What I do know is that, had I been allowed to pitch, it wouldn't have been long before I would have given in to the temptation to try the breaking stuff. Any kid would do the same. Like anybody else who has made it through the maze that leads to the major leagues, I've seen my share of lively young arms make the jump and then, in what seems like the blink of a fastball, burn out. There may not be the slightest connection to when they broke their first curve, but I often wonder. Did they reach the end of the line, long before their time, because they began the trip too early?

I think baseball and all who play it would be well-served by a detailed study on the subject. At most, it could save a lot of arms and, at least, prevent a little heartache.

Pitchin'

The spitter and other downright dirty deeds
a clean-living pitcher would never use

MAYBE IT SAYS SOMETHING about the society in which we live—maybe it says something about me, too—but there is much in baseball that appeals to those with a touch of larceny in their hearts.

Let them catch you putting the boot to a golf ball buried in something like the Mojave Desert, buster, and you'll never play the Masters. Nuzzle up to a punter after he nearly rams a football down your throat and they penalize your team fifteen yards and give his team the ball. Slip a couple of aces in your vest pocket and some guy named Wild Bill is bound to say, ''Draw, partner!'' and he sure as Boot Hill won't mean, ''Take another card.''

But baseball . . . hey, steal a hundred bases when a pitcher's back is turned and they put you on the cover of *The Sporting News*. And when the thief is out there at second base, he's busy tipping off his pal at the plate about what pitch the catcher is calling, where in the strike zone he wants it and if the poor guy on the mound has hub caps worth swiping.

Sure, they give the pitcher four balls to three strikes, but the hitter can foul off the best stuff he's got until Jim Acker comes home—which, as all Texas is aware, tends to be very, very late.

Corked bats. Blind umpires. Hitters who hang their laundry over the plate and cry all the way to first base when your batting practice fastball slips an inch or two inside. I could go on about the indignities heaped upon us, but pitchers having the stout hearts they do, we prefer to suffer in silence.

And get even.

Can you really blame a nice old guy—well, for the sake of argument, let's say a Don Sutton—if he gets a little better movement on his breaking stuff by nicking the ball with the eyelets of his glove? And when Rick Honeycutt was tossed out of a game a couple of seasons back after a tack was found in his glove, did anybody ask if it was planted? Sounds to me just like the sort of trick a hitter would play. When Dennis Martinez was with the Orioles, he used to hawk tobacco juice on his hands before he rubbed up a new ball, some say to make it darker, harder for the hitter to see. I think he might have been trying to compensate for all that dry air (snicker) in Baltimore.

Sure, the spitter is alive and well and flourishing in the major leagues. It's only been about sixty-five years since it was outlawed—to make the game more productive for the hitters, what else?—and if they made it legal again, I'd start using it tomorrow.

As pitches go, it is a thing of beauty. Or so I hear.

Actually, the term spitter is a misnomer. It might have been all right in the old days, when ballplayers were right up there in the social register with card sharks, whiskey runners and snake oil salesmen.

The preferred substance, at least the way I hear it, is a transparent jelly. There are any number of places where this substance can be secreted to avoid detection.

Gaylord Perry, alleged to have "wetted one up" on occasion, is said to have preferred a little streak of it along the seam on the right leg of his pants. Remember how he fiddled with his hat, ran his fingers across his brow, tugged on his ear and tucked the hair behind his ears? All sleight of hand. A smooth old pro like Perry would never make it so obvious. But, as he leaned forward for the catcher's signal, his right arm limp, he just might have collected the substance by brushing his first two fingers against the spot on the seam.

I've also been told of Vaseline being used, but the rub, (so to speak) is that it tends to soak into the uniform in later innings and leave a tell-tale stain. Certain brands of chewing gum produce a nice mix of goo and I understand that a trace of soap at the base of the neck becomes slick with a little sweat. Fail to wash behind your ears, as mom told you, and the gunk that builds beneath the lobes is said to work wonders on a baseball.

If I had a preference, it would be for good, honest sweat. It's natural. There's plenty of it. And who's going to stop you from wiping your brow? Fake the drying motion on the thigh area of the pants, but leave the first two fingers elevated and, consequently, slightly wet. Grip the ball so that neither the thumb nor the two moist fingers touch any of the seams. Throw it with the same motion as you would a fastball.

Since the dry thumb promotes traction and the wet fingers do quite the opposite, the effect is to minimize its rotation. I must have been AWOL the morning in Grade 3 that we unravelled the mysteries of aerodynamics, so I can't tell you the why of what happens next, but as the ball approaches the plate, it drops. Like off a table. Since the hitter is expecting an altogether different movement, there are generally two types of reaction. He swings mightily and misses, or he watches in wonder. Either one is acceptable to a pitcher.

If the umpire suspects, he rarely mentions it. Fact is, their record of law enforcement in this area is about as weak as a snapped jock strap. I'll bet you could count the number of times they've run a guy for this reason on one hand of Mordecai (Three-Fingered) Brown. If the hitter suspects, which is almost as rare, the ball is back in the pitcher's mitt and as dry as yesterday's toast before he says anything.

Given its wonderful properties, it is not a pitch one would use to excess. It probably would be best to save it for a jam and with two strikes on the batter. The last time I used it was in 1982. The last time I saw that ball, it was on its way to becoming a souvenir for someone in the bleachers at Municipal Stadium in Cleveland. Anyway, with the stuff I have, who needs to cheat?

I have an assortment of pitches but, without getting too technical, I depend on four of them—fastball, curve, slider, change-of-pace—which does not make me a whole lot different from other guys who play this game.

These numbers tell you how well I throw them: lowest cumulative earned run average in the American League, 1980–85 (3.07); toughest pitcher to hit, 1980–85 (.225 cumulative opposition batting average); club leader in wins (87), complete games (77), shutouts (19) and strikeouts (890).

I throw my best fastball, the one I grip along the seams, from ninety to ninety-four miles an hour. When it behaves, it tails by as much as a foot. It is best, therefore, to throw it to the middle of the plate and let it drift to the corners. My secondary fastball, gripped across the seams, remains true to its course and is usually spotted down and away on righthanded hitters, up and inside on lefthanded hitters. Make the mistake of throwing this one down the middle of the plate and you might as well hang a wreath on the mound.

My slow curve (seventy-eight to eighty-three m.p.h.) which I throw overhand (released at the one o'clock position) breaks straight down. My hard curve, in the high eighties, is released about 2:30 and breaks straight across. With a righthanded batter, for instance, I try to pick the outside corner with it or, when I have two strikes, toss it at him. The moment he thinks it might hit him, it breaks to the inside part of the plate. I like this pitch—but to make it effective, it must be used sparingly.

The slider, on the other hand, is the temptress of all pitches. Falling in love with it, which I did, is about as easy as falling off the mound. Master its intricacies—it breaks down and to the left, sharply in both cases, so there are two areas in which it can go awry—and you can swing the world by its tail.

It is thrown as hard as you would the fastball, but with a rotation far tighter than the curve. Its chief characteristic, where the hitter is concerned, is that the rotating seams appear to form a whirling red dot on the way to the plate.

To improve the grip, I sometimes scratch at the stitching on the ball to raise its seams. There are rules against "ragging," but they are rarely cited. The reason for this is that, although the manufacturers insist one baseball is the same as another, there is often a discrepancy in weight, seams and size.

The change-of-pace is, as the term implies, something to upset the timing of the hitter. In this category is a pitch I employ called the "dead fish." It is nothing more than a batting practice fastball, thrown at maybe fifteen to twenty miles slower than my best heater. For this reason, it also tends to drop as it approaches the strike zone.

As fine as all these pitches might be, they are not worth a tinker's dam if they are out of the strike zone. Right after your first pitching coach says, "How ya doin', kid," the next words out of his mouth are likely to be something about mechanics. For good reason, too.

What he's talking about are the three stages involved in delivering a pitch. Ignition: Both feet on the rubber, short step back with the left, raise hands above head. Coil: Hands come down, the body makes a quarter turn toward third base, the left knee tucks. Explosion: Stride to the plate, bring the arm around and release the ball.

Among the myriad factors that make it difficult is that, aside from maintaining precision in all three steps, each pitch requires a different release point. Be out by an inch in this area and it translates to feet by the time the ball crosses the plate. If you rush the lower body to the plate, it will force the upper body to catch up to the momentum, thereby messing up the release point.

The clearest example of this is when a pitcher, for some seemingly inexplicable reason, walks a batter on four pitches. If instinct hasn't told you the delivery or release point is out of kilter, the result will. When a pitcher is rattled for a couple of homers in the first inning, as I was one Saturday afternoon against the Minnesota Twins in September '85, and then sails through five innings, he has lost and then found his rhythm.

Compare it to the workings of a watch, if you like. If the flywheel is out of whack, it gains or loses time and, therefore, is ineffective. If the mainspring is busted, it fails to function and, therefore, needs a replacement part. Which is why baseball teams have bullpens.

Even when everything is working to peak capacity, as often happens with a younger pitcher with awesome but unrealized potential, things can go wrong.

The difference, and it tends to be more of a chasm than a gap, is what separates the thrower from the pitcher. Selection and its sharpness is achieved only with time.

In my mind, there is a book on every hitter I am likely to face on a given day. This one is weak on a curve low and outside. That one likes fastballs up. Generally speaking, the weakness is not geared so much to specific pitches, but rather to their location. Up or down, in or out. Experience is the teacher; how much the student benefits is up to him.

For the most part, selection is an instinctive process. The

key, in my mind, is not only a variety of pitches, but a variety of speeds. First time up, I might start him off with a hard fastball, a lazy curve and a slider. Second time around, I might use the same assortment in a different sequence. Curve, something hard, a changeup. Third time, just when he has me all taped, I'll go with still another sequence, except that I will stick with the pitch that gets him out until he proves he has learned to hit it.

It's called having a hole in your bat and, believe me, there are plenty who suffer from the affliction.

Among the prime examples who come to mind are Mitchell Page, formerly of the Oakland A's, and Steve Balboni and Buddy Biancalana of the Royals. Throw Page and Biancalana fastballs up and away and they will swing through them all day. Balboni's weakness is up and inside.

Defining the weakness is one thing; taking advantage is another. Balboni, who hits mistakes well, swatted a home run off me in K.C. in my second start this year when one of my pitches wandered into his area of strength.

In part, it suggests why I got off to such a disappointing start this season. It took me three games to find the rhythm that, for some reason, slipped away from me midway through spring training. Everything I threw seemed to cross the plate at the belt and thighs, nothing at the knees. Complicating matters was that the changeup, which was not performing, is not a pitch that can be abandoned. To get it working, I had to keep using it.

What sets apart the hitter who is consistently in the top ten (Brett, Boggs, Mattingly, et al.) is that they overcome their failings, or at least compensate for them. Each hitter has a pitch he knows is most likely to result in an out. He learns to hit it with moderate success or, unless it is the "pitch of decision" (a third strike), he learns to lay off. I might add that impatient hitters and "free swingers," those who ignore the strike zone, are among a pitcher's staunchest allies.

As complex as this might sound, I am prompted to say that one of the first bits of advice a pitching coach can impart to the budding pro is not to complicate things. Suits me. First, throw strikes. Second, get the hitter out. Third, don't let them score. I don't know how many pitchers I've seen get all messed up by plotting strategy with runners dancing off the bases.

"Don't think too much," Al Widmar keeps telling me. "It can be dangerous." For the most part, I take his advice.

As sly as all this might sound, however, a pitcher who wants to keep a grip on his peace of mind would do well to remember the immutable law that governs pitching.

You can fool all the hitters some of the time and some of the hitters all of the time, but you can't fool all of the hitters all of the time.

With thinking like that, a guy could get elected president.

Hittin'

*Brett, Boggs, Mattingly: There's only one way
to pitch to great hitters of the day . . . carefully*

MAKING IT TO THE MAJOR LEAGUES is only half of the battle.
Sticking around takes care of the other three quarters.

Yes, I am aware that what I just said doesn't come close
to adding up. Still, when I say that finding and keeping a job
in the majors demands an athlete give 125 per cent of himself, that's what I mean. And while we're at the old chalk-
board, I might add that one does not need a magna cum laude
in Sabremetrics to figure that the more a pitcher knows about a
hitter and his weaknesses, the better chance he has for a long
career.

Homework, as any dunce soon finds out, is a big part of
the job. Readin', 'ritin', 'n' 'rithmetic happen to be the ways
the club expects a pitcher to help out when he is between
starting assignments. Take a look at the dugouts the next time
you come to the ballpark and most likely you'll spot tomorrow's pitchers, pencils busy, hunched over their clipboards.
They're charting every pitch their man makes and what the
other team's hitters did with them. A lot of it is the same

stuff a kid in the stands scribbles on the program scorecard: who got the hits, who made the outs, who scored the runs. We're expected to take it a lot farther. Was the hit, out, strike, ball off a fastball (1), curve (2), slider (3), changeup (4)? At the knees, belt, letters? Inside, down the pipe, away?

All these facts and more, mind you, go into the charting of only one game, but you can see how a club builds a "book" over the years on hitters and their tendencies. This is put to use prior to the first game of every series we play, when manager Jimy Williams calls the team together and reviews the strengths and weaknesses of every hitter we are about to face. During the game, you might also notice hitting coach Cito Gaston, an outfielder for eleven seasons in the National League, shifting our defence according to the hitters' tendencies.

Next time you're at the ballpark, just to check how well we've done our homework, notice how often the fielder has to move only a few steps to catch the ball. Being at the right place at the right time, you'll find, is more than mere co-incidence.

For the price of my memoirs, which I trust is within the range of all who play in the major leagues, most managers and a few coaches, I'm not about to give away anything about the hitters I face that will come back to haunt me.

What I will say is that hitters like George Brett of the Royals, Wade Boggs of the Boston Red Sox and Don Mattingly of the New York Yankees get their share off me, just like they do everyone else. There are three sound reasons, and those who would scale these heights would do well to follow their example.

Unless a situation demands it—two outs, bottom of the ninth, down by a run—they do not, as a habit, swing for the fences. Since their stroke is more precise and, therefore, more controlled, they have a better chance of hitting the ball.

They must be selective. In every hitter's strike zone, there is a danger zone, a spot where he is most effective. Keep 'em high 'n' tight, low 'n' away, any sandlot pitching coach knows, and you'll stay out of trouble. Down the middle, at the buckle, better learn to duck. Though they are kept to a minimum at this level of the game, pitchers make mistakes and the hitter who waits and can take advantage of them is apt to become very rich indeed.

Considering the duress and the time frame within which they are forced to work, one must hold in awe the marvel of the machine that is man. A fastball that crosses the plate at ninety-four miles an hour, which is the speed at which some scouts have tracked mine, travels at 137.86 feet a second. Since the distance between the rubber on the mound and the plate is sixty feet, six inches, that gives the hitter all of 7/16ths of a second to do his work. To be successful at hitting a round ball with a rounded piece of wood, something the great Ted Williams once decreed the most difficult act in all of sport, the hitter must connect with a ''sweet spot'' on his bat that is the size of a dime.

It helps, too, if they are smart.

Hitters keep ''books'' on pitchers, too, and the best ones remember what they have ''read'' about his tendencies in a given situation.

By the time the 1980s are in the record books, it's my guess the historians will say that Brett was the hitter who dominated the decade. This will come as no big surprise to a lot of people who have seen him destroy the Jays (something like a career .375 batting average, 15 homers, and 75 RBI) through the seasons. When I think back to what he did to us, to me, in the playoffs last fall, my stomach flips.

The figures, in this case, don't lie. He was 8-for-23 (.339) at the plate in the seven games, including three homers and a pair of doubles, for five RBIs. He also reworked seven American League playoff records: hits (35), hits for extra bases (18), home runs (9), slugging percentage (.728), total bases (75), total runs (22), RBIs (19).

What makes him special—and I toss compliments around like manhole covers—is that there was no real hint of this potential when he was in the minors, where he never hit better than .300. It tells you that Brett had a good teacher and, more important, he was an exceptional student. In my book, that makes him smart. It's a lesson he has, pardon the pun, driven home a number of times at my expense.

The pitches that brought me to the major leagues are the slider, which I'm told (and believe) is among the best in baseball, and a fastball that, depending on how cranky it feels that day, darts in on a right-handed hitter and away from the leftie. Brett got fat and rich and happy hitting fastballs, in on him and away from him, up on him and down on him, so he gets no steady diet of them from me. Since he bats from the left side and I throw from the right, my slider cuts in on him and, therefore, across the danger zones. Let it hang and he will devour it.

For a while, I had a little success with curves and other offspeed stuff that upset his timing. Smart as he is, he adjusted.

Now it's at the point where I might get him out with any pitch and, yes, he might get a hit on any pitch. If there is a pattern to my pitch selection, it is that there is no pattern. Face him four times in an afternoon and you pitch him four different ways . . . all of them carefully. When he is on a tear, as he was early this season, it is safest just to walk him.

If Mattingly and Boggs have caused me less grief, it is because they have not been around as long. Like Brett, both hit from the left side, which allows them the same advantages facing a righthander like me. Like Brett, and unlike some other lefties I face who will remain nameless, they are quick to rectify any weak spots I might uncover.

Boggs is far less likely than the other two to hurt you with the long ball, but this is a small consolation when you

The wet look: *It was all the rage the day we captured the division title. Though I showered in champagne, I saved most of my celebrating for the playoff opener against the Royals.*

Man and boy: Seven years after I signed for $500 a month with the farm club in Dunedin, I was making $225 for every pitch I tossed for the Toronto Blue Jays.

To pitch or to hit; that was the big question.

To the rescue: *Some of my best friends, like Tom Henke, are firemen. Not only has he saved my day a number of times, but at 6-foot-5 he's a handy guy to have around during batting practice.*

Photo: Kevin Boland

The Canadian Duck? *As foursomes go, we were less than fearless during batting practice that day. With me are Rance Mulliniks, Jeff Burroughs and some guy the fans had nicknamed The Canadian Goose.*

Class of '59: *With Jesse Barfield, George Bell (left) and Lloyd Moseby (right) are the makings of the best outfield in baseball. The three of them were born within 15 days of each other in 1959.*

Stopped short: *What you don't see is the guy with the ball ready to pick off shortstop Tony Fernandez' glove, at left, the moment he tries to scoop it up. I'm ready to steal... towards second base.*

Back to the future: *Though pitching coach Al Widmar (left) wasn't part of the club at the time, this was the bullpen mound in Oakland where I first showed my stuff to the Blue Jays in the summer of '79.*

Mechanics: *As fine as a given pitch might be, it is worthless unless it can be thrown for a strike. Control is the key and it is the product of proper mechanics. A capable coach is a big help.*

Photos: Kevin Boland

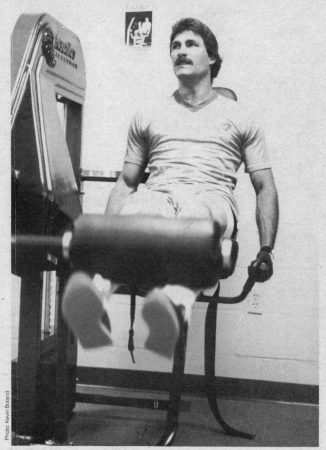

Working stiff: *One of the best things about baseball is that you can be a kid for twenty more years. The privilege, however, has a price. This is how it is paid.*

The first: *Willie Upshaw, with 104 RBIs in '83, was the first Jay to crack the century mark.*

Heavy hitter: *Cliff Johnson, one of the best two-strike hitters, waits his turn in the cage.*

Photo: Kevin Boland

Tough break: *Buck Martinez was on the outside looking in after breaking his leg in a play at the plate.*

Photo: Kevin Boland

Remember me? *Though I spent only a few weeks with the Chiefs, Syracuse fans remembered when the Blue Jays paid a visit.*

Full-time job: *After playing part-time for four seasons, Jesse Barfield got the job in right field last year. A teammate of mine at Dunedin in '78, he was named Blue Jays player of the year for 1985.*

The boss: *As much as Bobby Cox will say he had the men to do the job, it is no coincidence that in his four seasons with us, the club went from the bottom (78 – 84) to the top (99 – 62) in the AL East.*

Photo: Kevin Boland

Roughing the pitcher: *I hadn't seen a rush like this since I was a punter on the Oak Grove High football team. She made her move in the opener of the playoffs. Notice that I managed to hang onto the ball.*

We lose: *Reliever Bill Caudill and I both lost card partners this year. Gary Lavelle underwent arm surgery before the season started and Jim Acker followed Doyle Alexander and Bobby Cox to Atlanta.*

Easy does it: *When all about him were losing their heads in the AL East champions' champagne-soaked dressing room, Rance Mulliniks took time to think about the long, winding road he took to get there.*

Blue Jay for life: *General manager Pat Gillick (left) and Bob LaMonte, my financial adviser, held a news conference to announce the deal that tied me to the club for the rest of my career.*

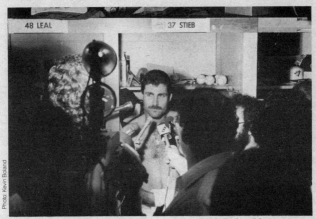

Press gang: *It is not a part of the game that I relish, but I have come to understand that the media has its job to do. If you're straight with them, I've found, they're pretty fair with you.*

Photo: Kevin Boland

Peewee prospect: *Andrew paid a visit to the clubhouse one day last summer when the club held a family picnic for the team. All the kids were given uniforms to match the ones their fathers wore.*

Much music: *Friend Geddy Lee of the rock band* **Rush** *jams with earnest amateurs, drummer Pattie and guitarist Dave.*

Pickin': *Killing time with one of my guitars in the recreation room of my house in Palm Harbor, Florida.*

Grinnin': *Andrew, the music critic in the house, offers his assessment of my efforts as I put away my toys.*

The home team: *Life on the road is not the barrel of fun some people think it is — especially with what's at home. Pattie, eight-month-old Ashley Danielle and four-year-old Andrew David.*

consider that at .325 in 1984, he had the worst of his four years as a hitter in the major leagues. He made up for his lapses in '85 by swatting 240 hits (42 doubles) and batting .368.

At first, I had a little luck when I discovered his liking for hard stuff inside that he could pull. Gave it to him, of course, but way inside so that the most damage he could do was a loud foul. Then threw him offspeed stuff outside that he'd tap to the right side of the infield. Prior to the Red Sox' visit to Toronto in June, I was winning the battle holding him to five singles in twenty-three confrontations for a .217 batting average. Boggs, however, beat me in other ways by drawing nine walks to boost his on-base average to .438.

Toward the end of last season, I began to notice in Mattingly a weakness against pitches up and away. It was a snippet of information I tucked away for reference in June when the Yankees paid the first visit of the '86 season to Exhibition Stadium. His first two times up, he doubled and singled and wound up scoring two runs. I also hear that some junkballers get to him by wasting a fastball away, then nibbling at the outside with slower stuff. With men on, he's smart enough to store the homerun swing and eat you alive by spraying hits to all fields. It shows in the numbers he has racked up against me. He was 12-for-33 (four doubles, two homers) for a .364 batting average and a .667 slugging average prior to the '86 season.

Brett, Boggs, Mattingly. There's only one rule to follow— pitch around them . . . if you can. All three of them are capable of being a big pain in the area of the hip pocket of American League pitchers, but the biggest little pain in that area of the uniform is Rickey Henderson of the Yankees. Except, in my case, for one thing. I can get him out, most of the time.

The primary reason is that both of us work from the right side and, therefore, he is forced to match his weaknesses (inside) with my natural strengths. You jam Henderson, pound him inside all day and lay the slider on the far side of the plate. You must get ahead in the count and then he'll help by swinging at pitches out of the strike zone, particularly below the knees.

A good thing, too. On the theory that an ounce of prevention is worth a pound of cure, keeping Henderson's fanny on the bench means this little nuisance won't rob you blind when your back is turned. There is still no way to steal first base.

Brett, Boggs, Mattingly. Call them swatters, if you will, but year in, year out, they beat on you with their singles and doubles all the way to the batting title. Sure, now and then a slugger will have his career year and win the triple crown (batting average, home runs, RBIs) but, in my book, it's the exception to prove the rule.

The next .400 hitter—I doubt there will be one but, with a little magic, Boggs is a threat—will have the same qualities that brought Brett (.390 in 1980) and Rod Carew (.388 in 1977) to the brink.

Patience. That word again. God grant me patience but, for God's sake, please do it now. It's a little saying that says a lot about a lot of hitters who might do themselves a lot of good if they acquired some of it.

To be successful, he must become a connoisseur of the pitcher's slip that puts a pitch into his area of strength. Ted Williams, who batted .316 for the Red Sox the year he turned forty-two, figured such an opportunity might arise once each time at the plate. Waiting sounds simple enough, I agree, but I've known hitters, good ones, who never saw a pitch they didn't like.

Since the mistake could be any one of half a dozen types of pitches, from a roundhouse curve to a split-fingered fastball, the hitter also has to be blessed with exceptional co-ordination of hand and eye. The quicker he picks up the flight of the ball—I'm convinced a guy like Brett locks in more quickly than the average hitter—the better the chance to put wood on it.

To hit from the left side is a distinct advantage, not only because most of the pitches he sees will come from the other side. The thrust of a lefthanded hitter is toward first base—and how many times has the instant replay shown us that half a step is the difference between a single and an out?

Still, for all of the foregoing, what fills the stands is the battle with the ripper. Forget what the purists say about the triple, the double play, and, yes, even the strikeout being what baseball is all about. It's the home run that yanks people out of their seats. Call it perverse, if you will, but depriving them of this treat for at least half an inning is how I get my kicks. The bigger the challenge, the more it pleases me when I succeed, the more it grates me when I fail.

Which brings me to Reggie Jackson. We go back a long way. Believe it or not, when I was a teenager in southern California, I was too involved in playing the game (and other pursuits) to take much notice of what was happening in the majors. Only when it was time for the World Series did I get really interested and, in those days, that meant Reggie, the Oakland A's and three Series titles.

To me, he was baseball; so, by extension, when he steps into the batter's box, nudges his specs back on the bridge of his nose and zings a few jets of tobacco juice my way, I know I have arrived.

I remember a time a few years back when, just like a wide-eyed rookie—which was not too far from the case—I went out to the batting cage to watch Jackson lose a few baseballs before he was to face me that night.

"Reggie," I said between cuts, "I've never struck you out."

"Never mind, you'll probably do it tonight."

I admit it surprised me a little that a great hitter like he is and had been was giving aid and comfort to the enemy, no matter how highly that adversary might regard him. There are times, too, when I talk until I think of something to say and this was one of them. "And hey," I said, "you've never taken me out of the park."

He smiled. Said nothing. Thinking back on it, I bet an alligator has the same expression before it makes a snack out of your arm.

It would happen for neither of us that night, though I've struck him out eight or nine times since then. And he hasn't taken me out of the park yet, but I get an eerie feeling whenever I think about that smile. I hope he's the forgetful type.

There are others besides Jackson in the league of big swingers. Just check the fine print in the sports pages. Over the years, I've been more successful than most in getting them out for the simple reason that I put a lot on a pitch and, generally, put it where I want it. The slugger, by the nature of his calling, does not have the bat control of a Brett, a Boggs, a Mattingly. Still, I make my share of mistakes and, when I do, I pay the same stiff price.

Even though my ratio of success is higher against the slugger, which makes getting them out a slightly more common experience, I still get the biggest charge out of doing it. Human nature, I guess, to want to inflict damage on the guy who wants to do the most damage to you.

If there's one confrontation that stands out, it has to be the session I had with Dave Kingman of the Oakland A's one night in Toronto a couple of seasons back.

The day before, Jim Gott, whom we traded to the San Francisco Giants for lefthander Gary Lavelle, ran a fastball off Kingman's ribs. I agree that all pitchers say it, but I know Gott had no intention of hitting Kingman. By the same token, I can sympathize with a hitter who gets a little miffed when it happens. Just the same, how many times do you see a hitter head out to the mound to commiserate with the pitcher who just tried to field a screaming line drive with his belly button? Accidents happen and hitters have a tendency to think that a pitcher's control is such that, with his eyes shut, he can hit a gnat in the ear whenever he chooses.

We were up a run late in the game the following night when Kingman, with little Joe Morgan on third, came to the plate. My first pitch, a slider I released a little early, sailed by his chin. He gives me a look designed to melt a pushy salesman. Second pitch, another slider, same place. He steps out of the box and glares. Like I just tried to cut in on him and the homecoming queen at the high school prom. Next pitch, fastball inside at the belt, and he begins to rave. "Go ahead," he howls. "Hit me."

By now, of course, the fans have picked up on this little drama and are howling for more. "If I want to hit you," I yell back at him, "I'll hit you."

Push has come to shove. Not only is it important for us that I keep him off first base—it is a cardinal sin to walk the potential winning run—but now personal pride is at stake. Now I have dug a big hole for myself. Kingman, with all the odds in his favor, wants to turn it into a grave.

Fastball, pretty much down the middle to tempt him, but up. He takes a wicked cut . . . and misses. Big noise in the stands. Next pitch, same pitch, same place. Big cut, big miss. Crowd comes to its feet.

It's crunch time. Miss now and I have egg all over my face. Slider, low and away, something totally different. He jumps on it, but fouls it straight back into the screen behind home plate. As innocuous as this might seem, what it tells a pitcher is that the hitter has missed his mark by maybe half an inch. Close call.

By now, the good folks of Buffalo, on the other side of Lake Ontario, should be able to hear the ruckus in Exhibition Stadium. As I rub up a new ball, I'm thinking that, save for one pitch, I've thrown everything but the resin bag at him.

How about a nice, fat, juicy fastball right down the middle. Strength against strength. Mad Bomber vs. The Big Bazooka.

Swing and a miss.

For Kingman, his head bowed and his bat trailing, it was a long walk back to the dugout. I looked over my shoulder as I trotted off the field, waited for some snappy comeback to occur to me, and then it dawned on me. The fastball, my old pal, had said it for me.

Star Wars

*The lesson Sutter taught me at the '81 All-Star Game
was the one The Strikeout King paid for in '85*

I'M A NEAT GUY.

Now don't go getting the idea that I think I'm something
more than special, especially after I've spilled a ton of ink in
this book trying to deflate the overblown image some people
have of me. Nor am I saying that I'm one of those dandies
who can't walk out of the john without my moustache waxed,
my gold chains glowing and the tassles on my loafers knot-
ted just so . . .

Give me a clean shirt, jeans and sweatsocks fresh from
the laundry, a pair of designer sneakers and I figure I'm fit
for the street. On the road, of course, the team has a dress
code and, since we are considered representative of the organization, I have no quarrel with wearing jacket and tie, slacks
and shined shoes. On the field, though the uniform is the
same for all, each of us brings to it his individual stamp. The
tilt of the cap, sleeve length of the dark blue undershirt, how
much white hose to show beneath the stirrup socks, even the
way we tie the laces over or under the fold of the tongue in

our spikes. Nit-picky things, the kind of stuff in which a head doctor might find hidden messages, but, like I say, I'm a neat guy.

Imagine, then, my shattered sense of decorum that August night of '81, when the opportunity to become a footnote in baseball history seized me by my slumbering desire to be a hitter in the major leagues.

And what a setting!

There were 72,086 in the stands at Municipal Stadium in Cleveland that night, largest crowd ever to see the All-Star Game, and maybe fifty million more gathered before their TV sets. Manager Jim Frey called me out of the bullpen in the eighth after Mike Schmidt's two-run homer had given the Nationals a 5-4 lead. I got the next two guys and, as I pondered my selection of pitches in the top of the ninth, Frey wandered over and told me I would have to hit for myself in the bottom of the inning.

Come again?

Simply put, because Tony Armas had been called to run for Fred Lynn after he banged up his knee sliding into second base earlier in the game, Frey had exhausted his supply of hitters. My first thought was to wonder how I would get the next three outs. My next thought, like Cinderella going to the ball, was to wonder what I would wear.

Imagine my chagrin, neat guy that I maintain I am, going to the plate wearing a Seattle Mariners helmet borrowed from Tom Paciorek, gloves from Rick Burleson of the California Angels and a bat from Mike Squires of the Chicago White Sox.

No wonder I was such a disaster at the plate. With all this strange haberdashery to befuddle me, never mind that I hadn't picked up a bat in anger for years, what match was I for Bruce Sutter and his famous forkball?

Imagine a fellow pitcher—even if he does happen to work in that other league—using so devastating a weapon against one of his own. Given the same circumstances, certainly I would have shown him my slider, sort of a souvenir for the guys back in St. Louis, but professional courtesy dictated a few garden-variety fastballs for me to wave at as they went by.

But the forkball! This is an awesome pitch and, I must say, difficult to control since the grip requires that the ball be wedged between the first two fingers. It behaves similarly to the outlawed spitter, dropping suddenly and darting left or right at the last moment. It is common knowledge, in fact, that a pitcher who adds ''the wet one'' to his repertoire often says the new pitch is nothing but the old forkball.

Maybe with all this strange hitter's gear I was wearing, maybe by the way I carried myself—after all, I had been a fair hitter during my college days—I frightened Sutter into thinking I was the real thing. The first forkball he sent my way that night looked like it fell off the dinner table. I waved at it. Since I was able to foul off the next one, Sutter some day might be able to persuade me it was something other than the forkball, but the third one definitely was his best Sunday pitch. As I waited for it, I thought to myself that the ultimate embarrassment would be to let it go for a called third strike. This, thank heavens, was not to be. I struck out swinging.

It was a cruel lesson that I carried with me for four long years and put into effect at the '85 All-Star Game in Minneapolis. (Well, hell, I have to think of some excuse for treating Nolan Ryan so shabbily in Minneapolis last summer.) While Ryan is a man whose deeds as a pitcher (4,100 strikeouts and counting) I envy, his feats as a hitter (.123 career average) were no threat to the folks in the cheap seats at the Metrodome that night. He came to the plate in the eighth inning with nothing much at stake since the Nationals, as usual, were about a touchdown ahead.

Blame it on Ernie Whitt, my batterymate from Toronto,

who was making his first appearance in an All-Star Game. He ordered two wicked fastballs and, figuring we had Ryan primed for another, called for a slider. It was a little better than I intended, kicking up dirt as it broke over the plate, and Ryan waved at it for the third strike. Even though I had suffered a similar fate years before, I felt a flicker of guilt that Ernie could show such insensitivity in his selection. The consolation, I guess, is that I had struck out my ninth all-star in as many innings and, since no one has done it more than Ryan, Ernie thought it appropriate that we ring him up.

Which brings me to my shining moment as a hitter and pitcher in what the sportswriters call "the midsummer classic." I like to think the one helped set up the other that July evening in '83 at Comiskey Park.

That I had been invited to the game in Chicago was an honor, considering that fifty years ago to the day, the American League had won the first All-Star Game at the very same park. That manager Harvey Kuenn picked me to start gave me an idea of what baseball immortality means. For a while, with nineteen oldtimers still left from that first game watching this fresh kid try to steal their thunder, I wondered if it all would turn out to be a cruel joke.

Steve Sax of the Dodgers, leading off for the Nationals, topped a ball to my left that I pounced on in a flash and coolly proceeded to throw ten feet over the head of first baseman Rod Carew. Next batter, Tim Raines of the Expos, hit another one back at me. I fielded it and threw a perfect strike to first. Carew, blinded by the evening sun glancing through the stadium archways, never saw it. Sax scored and Raines scooted to third.

About this time, I was wondering if Harvey was on the bullpen telephone and ordering a couple of wallbangers from room service. Time to go to work. Andre Dawson watched a third strike, Al Oliver walked, Dale Murphy fanned and Mike Schmidt struck out swinging.

With the score 1–1 heading into the bottom of the second —after I retired Gary Carter, Ozzie Smith and Mario Soto— my turn at the plate came up. With none out, Dave Winfield (double) on third and Manny Trillo (error) at first, I stepped into the box. Visions of a home run flashed before my eyes as I looked down to the coach's box at third base for the sign.

Bunt.

So I laid it down, perfectly, and Trillo scampered to second. Soto walked Carew intentionally to load the bases and, with Robin Yount's fly to center field, Winfield romped home with the lead run.

I breezed through the third inning and in our half we scored a record seven runs, four of them on Fred Lynn's smash to right field, the first grand-slam in all-star history.

One tainted run, for which I can blame myself, no hits, four strikeouts and a walk. Good enough for the American League's first win, after eleven consecutive losses, since '71 in Detroit. Not a bad night's work, if I do say so myself. At the same time, now that I look back on it, it tells me how quickly things can change.

A year later, at gusty Candlestick Park in San Francisco, I achieved the distinction of starting my second All-Star Game in a row. To be honest, my mind was not as focused as it should have been on the task at hand.

I remember taking my seat in the dugout after warming up, feeling cold and a little bit alone even though my family and high school friends were in the stands, and watching the wind sweep the park and send scraps of paper swirling across the infield. I thought about Willie Mays playing here for fifteen seasons, his power betrayed by currents that gobble up most everything to left field, and marvelled at how he managed to hit 450 home runs in that period. I wondered how many bleacher seats he would have wrecked at Exhibition Stadium.

My grandfather, railroad man John Meeler, had died of

cancer the previous week and we had buried him only the day before. How often, through the years, had he reprimanded me for issuing too many walks? Nobody rode for free on his train. There are times, to this day, when I hear that gentle, chiding voice after I have issued yet another pass. To top it off, my former agent and I would haggle over money before an arbitrator for a couple of days following the game.

It was a long week.

I gave up a run in each inning, including the only one earned in five all-star appearances, and took the loss in our 3–1 defeat. Tip of the cap to Dwight Gooden and Fernando Valenzuela, who struck out six in a row.

The happiest I ever have been at an All-Star Game, purely because it was my first, was the one in '80 at Los Angeles. My parents, brother and a flock of friends from school days drove down from San Jose and, during the festivities, I got to meet comedian Jonathan Winters, who is a particular favorite of mine.

I admit to experiencing a sense of culture shock in the hours leading up to the game. The way I remember it, as far as most fans outside of Toronto were concerned, we were a family team. Dave Who? Lloyd Who? Alfredo Who? Now I was in a dressing room that housed the Who's Who of the game. No need to recite the names here, of course, but the one that fascinated me was Reggie Jackson, whose exploits I had followed when he was the straw that stirred the drink (and other stuff) with the Oakland A's.

Rookie type that I was, I was dressed, shaved and powdered an hour before I needed to be. Jackson, whose locker was right next to mine, was fashionably late. My big dilemma was thinking up an excuse for going back to my stall, rooting through my stuff and hoping he might take notice. Maybe he remembered what it was like to be a rookie, because I no sooner made my move than Jackson looked up and began talking to me like I was a long-lost pal who had finally come home. In the middle of a season in which he would hit forty-one homers and bat .300 for the Yankees, he could have played the star for a wide-eyed kid. He didn't and, as surely as it taught me something about him, it set an example I would follow whether or not I came anywhere near approaching his type of success on the field.

Since every team in the majors must send a representative to the game, it occurred to me that I might spend the evening purely as a spectator. Manager Earl Weaver sent my heart into my mouth when he sent me out to conserve a 3–2 deficit in the late innings. To my distinguished list of credits, a hyperactive slider added another. I tied an all-star record with two wild pitches in the seventh inning. I was also nicked for two walks and an unearned run, the final marker in a 4–2 loss to the Nationals.

Still, I considered I had not made a fool of myself and that I had represented my team well. I was hoping that I would be invited back again.

Soon.

Sign of the Times

Wait Till Next Year, said the sheet in the bleachers
but wasn't Opening Day a little early to hang it?

DENIS MENKE GOT AROUND.

He broke in with the 1962 Braves, when Milwaukee was in the National League, moved with them to Atlanta in '66, was traded to the Houston Astros in '67, the Cincinnati Reds in '71 and back to Houston in '74. He played in 1,598 games, two championship playoffs and one World Series. In 13 seasons, he performed in 841 games at shortstop, 420 at third base, 233 at second, 162 at first and 5 in the outfield.

You could look it up in *The Baseball Encyclopedia*.

In his time, he was in lineups that featured some of the finest who ever played the game. Henry Aaron, Eddie Matthews and Warren Spahn with the Braves; Joe Morgan with the Houston Astros; Pete Rose, Johnny Bench and Tony Perez with the Reds.

When he is remembered, however, it is often as part of a trade between the Reds and Astros in the autumn of '71. Lee May, Tommy Helms and Jimmy Stewart went to Houston for Menke, Morgan, Ed Armbrister, Cesar Geronimo and pitcher Jack Billingham. Highway robbery. The Big Red Machine was ready to roll.

What Denis Menke will not be remembered for, what he well might like to forget, were his days on manager Bobby Mattick's coaching staff in the summer of '81. The very nature of the job demands that a coach have the eyes of a .350 hitter in searching for the positive upon which to build a team. One night toward the end of the season, in keeping with the code of the eternal optimist, he told the troops, "What we need is the feeling that when we get ahead in a game, we're going to win it. What we've been doing is wondering how we're going to lose."

That's the way it was in the summer of '81. Not a whole lot different, now that you mention it, from '79 and '80, my first two seasons in Toronto.

Diplomacy forces me to say the best move we made in '81 was to go on strike for forty-six games. At the time, our record was 16–42. This, one of the goons in the press box wrote, had put us on course for a 45–117 season—if we didn't go into a slump.

I will admit it was a team effort.

Not one hitter came within forty points of a .300 average and the club's aggregate was .226, the worst in all of baseball and a good twenty points less than the rest of the American League. The pitching was also less than spectacular, with nine of the other thirteen teams posting better ERAs than our staff's 3.82.

For the most part, for reasons I consider as obvious as a whiff of Jim Acker's aftershave, the '79 and '80 seasons were written off as "building years" for the club. That's a term general managers use to persuade the fans to be patient with the motley crew of long-in-the-tooth veterans and greener-than-grass kids while he engineers the miracle that will produce a contender.

In '79, the club's third season in the American League—

manager Roy Hartsfield's last on the field after a lifetime in the game—we compiled the worst record in baseball (53–109) and finished our customary dead last in the East Division. The bright spot was shortstop Alfredo Griffin, who batted .287 and set club records for hits (179), runs (81), and stolen bases (21). He was named Rookie of the Year, but even that was tainted when a tie (John Castino, Minnesota Twins) was declared for the first time in league history. Our power was first baseman John Mayberry (.279, 21 HR, 74 RBI) but what says it all is that this team, playing half its games in one of the friendliest parks for hitters, was the only one in the majors to crack less than one hundred home runs.

The pitching? Put it this way. In three seasons (54–107, 59–102, 53–109) the staff had been rung up for 318 losses. Cy Young, who won 511 games in his career with second-rate clubs, took 22 years to lose 313. At 8–8 (4.33 ERA) in half a season, I was the club's only pitcher without a losing record, but I had to prove I could get through the league a second time.

Under Bobby Mattick, the club made strides in 1980, losing less than one hundred games (67–95) for the first time. The Seattle Mariners (59–103), our cousins in the '77 expansion, had reclaimed the title of worst team in baseball. Mayberry hit thirty homers (82 RBIs) and there were names in the lineup (Damaso Garcia, Lloyd Moseby, Garth Iorg) that would become familiar to the fans in Toronto.

The pitching, with Jim Clancy at 13–16 (3.30 ERA) and me at 12–15 (3.70), seemed to be coming around—flirting, we even dared to hope, with respectability in '81.

How ridiculous did it get?

We're up 2–1 in the bottom of the eighth in Oakland one day in May, I have a two-hitter and only one of the last sixteen A's has reached base. I am sailing. With one out, Rob Piciollo singles politely to center, but takes two more bases on Barry Bonnell's bid for a shoestring catch. He scores on a sacrifice fly and up comes Rickey Henderson, who pops a single to right on a 1–2 pitch, then promptly steals second base.

Out comes Bobby Mattick. I know why. He will try to calm me, remind me first base is open and that walks don't always kill ya, all the while giving the 'pen a few more pitches to get ready. "Son," he says, "don't give Murphy a pitch down the middle."

Murphy hits the next pitch, down the middle, for a base hit to center field. Another run. I walk Jim Spencer on four pitches. On a 0–2 pitch, I hit Wayne Gross. Bases loaded. Tony Armas singles for two runs. I'm gone. As I bang my head against the wall of the shower, Mitchell Page singles off reliever Jackson Todd for another run. Oakland 6, Toronto 2.

I couldn't see it at the time, but given a couple of seasons to develop, there were days when Mattick's lineup would have been very much at home when we won the East Division last year. Whitt or Martinez catching; Jim Clancy, Luis Leal or me pitching; Willie Upshaw at first, Damaso Garcia at second, Garth Iorg at third, Alfredo Griffin at short; George Bell, Lloyd Moseby, Barry Bonnell and Alvis Woods in the outfield. We were young, but the second half of the '81 season produced a mark of 21–27, still last in the East, but only 7½ games off the pace.

I finished with an 11–10 record (3.18 ERA), not nearly as respectable as I would have liked, and I expected to spend a long winter festering over (real or imagined) slights in my attempt to get my fair share of the bankroll.

It was a matter of record in the spring of '81 that the club, which had operated on a bankroll of $850,000 its first season, was now spending $2.8 million. John Mayberry, who could have filed for free agency, got the biggest chunk at $800,000. Jim Clancy, who could have filed for arbitration, signed for $200,000. Since I could do neither, I was told to whistle when I asked for four times the $155,000 I drew in

'80. Four days after the pitchers and catchers reported for spring training, the club renewed my contract at $85,000.

Did I think I was being had? The next spring, when I did not qualify for arbitration, I had this to say: "They don't want to pay me. The organization is just too cheap. I've been very bitter over the last couple of years. I can take them to arbitration next year, but what I'm really hoping for is a trade so I won't have to go through that hassle."

As I mentioned earlier, there were certain dynamics at work during this period of my life that tended to make me shoot first and ask permission later. Dredging up the hard feelings here is done solely to suggest the stresses under which I worked that season.

With five straight losses to wind up the '80 campaign and having been shut out in my pitch for a hefty raise, I figured I had a right to expect my luck to change on the field. It did. It got worse.

I was 0–3 before most Canadians had parked their dogsleds for the summer and, in twenty-one innings I pitched, my side had not scored a run.

As the newspaper stiffs gathered around my locker, following the loss to the Milwaukee Brewers that made it eight in a row for me, I made an attempt at gallows humor. "I'm not going to worry," I told them. "I know I'm going to win one time or another. The big question is whether I have to wait four or five years to do it." It would never do to admit it, but the prospect of matching Tom Underwood's club record of thirteen losses in a row was very much on my mind. "My first year I won a lot of games here," I said. "Last year, I won most of them on the road. Maybe I should try pitching on the border."

Or in Yankee Stadium, before 50,000 New York fans who turned out to attend Viet Vets Day. It was no walk through Central Park. We won it 2–1, Lloyd Moseby scoring the winning run on the front end of a double steal in the third inning. Big conference in the eighth inning (man on second, Reggie at the plate) but we pitch to him and he pops out.

Bring on the Baltimore Orioles, the one team I had yet to beat, the club that trashed me 6–1 in my major-league debut.

Revenge, I discovered quickly, has its own schedule. By the time I got the hook in the fourth inning at Baltimore, I had tossed 74 pitches (40 balls) and walked six but, having stranded seven runners, I proved I was as good at getting out of trouble as I was getting into it. They won 4–3, the bullpen taking the loss.

Back in Toronto, with Buck Martinez behind the plate for the first time, I finally achieved my victory (5–2, four hits) over the Orioles. Martinez doubled off Jim Palmer in the fifth to tie it 2–2 and scored the winner on a double by Alfredo Griffin.

Frustration reclaimed its grip in Cleveland, a 1–0 loss to the Indians in which I threw a six-hitter, then tightened it again in a 6–2 debacle against the Oakland A's, and was capped by a 4–1 pasting the Texas Rangers hung on me in Toronto early in June.

Frankly, if a strike had to be, it was coming at the right time for me. With our record at 16–42 and dropping like one of Gaylord Perry's spitters, the selfish side of me prepared for a long layoff.

We were back in August and, with the benefit of a split-season formula that set up playoffs to decide division winners, Toronto got its first faint whiff of pennant fever. For the record, though it had been rigged by the strike, we were not eliminated until the last month of the season.

Three incidents in that summer of '81, in their unique and curious ways, put it in perspective.

Late in September, all hope having long since evaporated, we got involved in a marathon (seven hours, eighteen minutes) doubleheader with the A's. I had pitched nine frames of the thirteen-inning opener that we lost 3–2 and was on the bench when, with our lineup depleted, Danny Ainge was sent in at shortstop for Oakland's last at-bats. Ainge, after three seasons with the club, decided his future in pro sport lay in another game, another town. As he took up his position, a basketball floated out of the stands and bounced neatly into his hands. Danny Two-Sport had a way out and a sympathetic Toronto was saying its goodbye.

The second incident, though couched in acrimony, ended with one of the funnier lines I have heard in the game. At the same time, it reflected the frustration we felt after four seasons as the doormats of baseball.

I had a running feud with Ferguson Jenkins of the Texas Rangers, a pitcher with the Hall of Fame credentials I would be happy to list after my name, based on his belief that I hit some of his teammates on purpose. After a game we lost late in August, the newspaper guys congratulated Jenkins on his work. "Whoopee," he dead-panned, "anybody can beat Toronto."

The following week, Toronto beat him 3–0. Though two of my pitches hit Buddy Bell and Mario Mendoza, Texas manager Don Zimmer had ordered him not to retaliate. In the Texas clubhouse, Jenkins swore revenge, despite suggestions that he might be better served focusing his anger on a .350 hitter.

Buck Martinez, who heard the story a few minutes later, said with a straight face, "He'd have to hit two of our guys to do that."

The last incident, the first in a way, happened on Opening Day in Toronto. High in the bleachers behind left field there was a banner, what once might have been one of mom's best white sheets. On it, scrawled in blue paint, were the words, "Wait Till Next Year."

This One's for Me

Nothing wrong with looking out for Number 1
as long as you don't forget the team comes first

SHOW ME A GOOD LOSER and I'll show you someone who has become good at losing.

Sure, I agree the world would be a better place by far if, as the rhyme by Grantland Rice suggests, it mattered not whether you won or lost, but how you played the game. My regrets, therefore, go out to all who think I ought to be just as delirious after having the Schlitz beaten out of me as when I've had the grandest time beating it out of someone else. The sad fact is that, even when you're a kid, they keep score for the sole purpose of telling the difference between the winners and the losers. It is the way of things, an instinct as intrinsic as survival, to want to be good, to want to be better, to want to be best.

Among the beauties of the game that consumes my efforts, perhaps the one that appeals to my very essence, is that there is a winner and a loser on every pitch. Add up these little triumphs and tragedies and, if the sum is failure, then it is as basic as hunger that I will feel sore about it.

If I tend to show it more than the next guy and if that

means I'm a poor loser, then I'll make my apologies to the first person I meet, whomever that might be, on the other side of the grave. Having said as much, it should come as no great shock that I want to win every award—with the exception of Comeback Player of the Year—that major league baseball affords the pitcher.

So when I get jobbed, as I was following the 1982 season by the good folks who write about baseball, it is not part of my sensitive nature to keep it to myself.

That was the year that Pete Vuckovich of the Milwaukee Brewers won the Cy Young Award as "the best pitcher" in the American League. That was the year I finished fourth in voting by members of the Baseball Writers' Association of America. What strikes me as curious is that *The Sporting News*, whose pages are filled each week by BBWAA writers, named me American League Pitcher of the Year for '82. And I don't care if they did misspell my name on the plaque they sent me.

The Cy Young Award, named after the man who won 511 victories between 1890 and 1911, was inaugurated in 1956 by former commissioner Ford Frick to honor "the best pitcher" in baseball. The first to win it was Don Newcombe of the Brooklyn Dodgers. Among others who were celebrated are Steve Carlton of the Philadelphia Phillies, four times; Sandy Koufax of the Los Angeles Dodgers, three times; Tom Seaver when he was with the New York Mets, three times; Jim Palmer of the Baltimore Orioles, three times; Denny McLain of the Detroit Tigers, twice; Gaylord Perry, twice, with the San Diego Padres and the Cleveland Indians; Warren Spahn of the Milwaukee Braves; Early Wynn, with the Chicago White Sox; Whitey Ford of the New York Yankees; Bob Gibson of the St. Louis Cardinals; and Catfish Hunter, with the Oakland A's. If, in the recital of this partial list, you get the impression that this would be pretty good company to seek out, then we think along similar lines. When I was deprived of it in 1982, you bet I was upset.

The case, your honor, is predicated on the fact that the award is supposed to go to "the best pitcher" in the league. Therefore, let us examine the facts. I won 17 and lost 14 that season, with an earned run average of 3.25. In 38 starts, I led the American League in complete games (19), innings pitched (288⅓) and shutouts (5). I gave up 271 hits, struck out 141 and walked 75.

Vuckovich, one of the originals with our club back in '77, won 18 and lost 6, with an ERA of 3.34. He finished nine of 30 starts, with one shutout, gave up 234 hits in 223⅔ innings, struck out 105 and walked 102.

Hands down, he had the better W–L record. Also hands down, considering the team behind him, he should have better numbers. The Brewers, under manager Harvey Kuenn, finished first in the East with a 95–67 record. Our club finished last, tied with the Cleveland Indians, at 78–84. Harvey's Wallbangers, as they were called, walloped 216 home runs and led the league with a .455 slugging percentage.

Their everyday lineup was, in a word, awesome. Shortstop Robin Yount (.331 batting average, 29 home runs, 114 runs batted in), first baseman Cecil Cooper (.313, 32 HR, 121 RBI), third baseman Paul Molitor (.302, 19 HR, 71 RBI), center fielder Gorman Thomas (.245, 39 HR, 112 RBI), left fielder Ben Oglivie (.244, 34 HR, 102 RBI), catcher Ted Simmons (.269, 23 HR, 97 RBI). We were in the "building stage" and it showed in the numbers we put on the board: 110 fewer homers and 240 fewer runs scored than the Brewers. Our big guns, just finding the range in the majors, were first baseman Willie Upshaw (.267, 21 HR, 75 RBI), right fielder Jesse Barfield (.246, 18 HR, 58 RBI), center fielder Lloyd Moseby (.236, 9 HR, 52 RBI) and second baseman Damaso Garcia (.310, 42 RBI and 44 stolen bases).

To say I was robbed in the Cy Young voting would (mildly) overstate the case. Just the same, the terms of the award dictate that it should go to "the best pitcher" in the league. I think even Mr. Young would agree that a winning record isn't what it is all about. After all, while he was setting an unassailable mark of 511 victories, he also was losing a record 313 times.

Disappointed as I might have been at the tendency of the typewriter jockeys to go with a front runner, I cannot say I was all that surprised. It was the final chapter of an unsettling season. Fact is, as I look back upon the summer of '82, I have a little difficulty recognizing the central character in these memoirs.

Ask anyone who follows baseball closely and they will tell you that the uncommon tends to become the common in the unfolding of a season. So it was with me in '82 and much of it—giving up 27 homers, for instance, when I had run up a total of 33 the previous three seasons—I found less than gratifying.

It began for me in a purple rage over the club's salary offer and it was fuelled by strong talk in New York that the Yankees were eager to have me. "It's great that other clubs want me," the diplomatic Mr. Stieb told the papers, "but it doesn't do much good unless they follow through. I wouldn't think Toronto would have a very high asking price, since they aren't willing to pay me much. They have no respect for me."

There have been times when I talked until I thought of something to say and times when, having had my fill of one set of toes, I'd open my mouth and start nibbling on the other foot. Sometimes, I've managed to do both at the same time.

We were three weeks into the season before I recorded my first victory, 7–0 at Kansas City, and not before I had blown a 7–1 lead at Boston a couple of weeks earlier to lose 8–7.

I remember my first loss to the Chicago White Sox—Greg Luzinski nailed a low fastball into the left field seats for a three-run homer and a 4–3 victory—and cussing out Buck Martinez, for all of Comiskey Park to see, for calling the wrong pitch. I remember blowing a no-hitter in the seventh at Oakland because I shook off Gino Petralli three times (fastball, slider, curve) to serve Tony Armas a two-strike changeup that he smoked into the seats in left field. "I played against him all winter," Gino told me later. "He sits on the changeup, especially when he's behind in the count."

It was a season, too, that paid heed to history. In an 8–1 pasting by the A's in June, I watched Armas set a major-league record by recording eleven outs in right field and another for total chances when he tossed out a runner at second base. For the first time in my career, in a 4–2 loss to the Yankees in August, I gave up three homers in one game (Dave Winfield, Ken Griffey, Roy Smalley). Rookie Gary Gaetti of the Twins, a .197 hitter that Sunday we celebrated July 4th in Minneapolis, lit a firecracker of his own on my first pitch of the ninth for a 4–3 loss.

To be sure, I had my moments. I remember the 9–2 walloping we gave the K.C. Royals and nemesis Larry Gura; the 4–0 conquest of the Red Sox, on two hits, one hot August night in Toronto; the 4–2 squeaker (three runs in the ninth) over the Brewers in Milwaukee the next week; the 2–0 triumph over Seattle, on four hits, for my seventeenth win of the season and nineteenth complete game.

Time and the season's effort had not blunted my sense of decorum when it came to discussing the merits of a club that had shown signs (fifty-eight games decided by one run) of major improvements. "I've resigned myself to making the best of a bad situation," I told the newspaper guys. "I don't like being here. I've wasted three years up here. I'd like to go somewhere with a contender. Today. That's the big thing. Today.''

Don't sugar-coat it, Dave. Get off the fence. Tell 'em exactly what you think. Call it desire, if you're in a mood to be kind, a not-so-charming byproduct of my search for individual excellence that I think can be channelled into the success of a team.

More than any sport, in my opinion, baseball is a team game played by the individual. Look for a crowd on the diamond—the mark of any team sport, be it football, basketball, ice hockey or soccer, is a cluster of humanity—and the most you will find is three at home plate, one of them being the umpire. Pitcher versus hitter is the most solitary of battles in sport, yet no confrontation is more pivotal to success for either team. And yet, as alone as the pitcher be, he must rely on eight of his teammates to make the outs. The catcher hangs on to the third strike. Infielders scoop up ground balls and throw them to the first baseman. Outfielders track down fly balls.

Curious, isn't it, that the pitcher records the fewest putouts in a game?

As singular as the efforts of the participants tend to be, even though they are tuned to a common goal, it stands to reason that the striving for individual recognition is for the collective good.

Doing it for yourself is a concept considered alien to team sport, but baseball can be something of an exception so long as such efforts do not become paramount to the individual. Obviously, a hitter who protects his average by coming down with a case of twenty-four-hour flu should turn in his tutu. The same goes for a pitcher who develops a twinge in his elbow the night he is to face Murderers' Row. By far, the majority of players are willing to sacrifice all and, in so doing, have every right to hope for the rewards for selfless efforts. If it weren't so, the establishment would not pay such handsome bonuses for making the All-Star team, pitching a certain amount of innings, the Cy Young Award and, yes, even the Gold Glove.

Which reminds me . . .

The Gold Glove Award, one for each position, is awarded to the player a panel of judges feels was the league's best fielder throughout the season.

There were times early in my career when I thought I had a shot at winning it but, every year, the voters seemed mesmerized by the Orioles' elegant Jim Palmer. No big deal. I figured the vote could have gone either way and, since old Aches 'n' Pains had been around longer, he had the edge on the familiarity factor.

The '84 season has to be a different story. I made two errors, both on pickoff attempts at second base, and Ron Guidry of the Yankees made none. That alone might appear decisive except that at 195⅔ innings, he pitched 71⅓ fewer than my league-leading 267 and, therefore, had fewer chances. Given the fact that he is a lefthander, the pickoff play at first is a far simpler matter for him in that he does not have to pirouette.

I realize it might be a pain in the pencil sharpener, but it would be fairer if the judges had stats on the number of chances taken—a wild throw is counted an error, an accurate throw counts for nothing—as well as the number of assists and putouts a pitcher contributes.

If it were for glovework alone, the figures say I'm a contender (hands down, so to speak) every year. With two fielding errors over seven major-league seasons—I've made my share of sloppy throws—it would be oh so trite if I said I didn't think I fielded my position as well as anyone. The same would apply if I said it didn't bother me when I botch that one play.

It happened one night last August when we were playing the Cleveland Indians at Exhibition Stadium. Shortstop Julio Franco hit a high hopper to my right. I had to run down the back of the mound, but I fielded it cleanly. Haste makes waste and I had trouble getting a grip on it for the throw. Finally, when I did, I just dropped it. Dammit. E-1. Get the mirror out, Ham Hands, and see what others see when Stieb glares.

It is not merely to save face, which I admit is a consideration, that I have worked long and hard to enhance my ability in the field. Fortunately for me, I played a bit of shortstop in my time, so I got plenty of practice.

There is also an element of preservation involved. Officially, the distance between plate and mound is sixty feet, six inches but, after I've stretched in delivery, that shrinks to about fifty-four feet. The only player closer to the hitter is the catcher and he's wearing an iron mask, chest protector and shin guards.

The first rule is to be in the best position possible to field whatever comes back at you. That means facing the batter, on your toes but not off balance, glove open at the waist and the free hand nearby. The reflexes of a cat, the eye of the eagle, these are great gifts. When they are impaired, as they can be by a sloppy delivery, then you'd better have a couple of ribs to spare and a high tolerance for pain.

Or worse.

Herb Score was twenty-four years old and, after a 20–9 record for the Cleveland Indians in 1956, they were casting a plaque for him in Cooperstown. In May of 1957, Gil McDougald of the Yankees lined one of Score's ninety-five m.p.h. fastballs back at him. Though the sight of his eye was saved, and it was a near thing, Score was never the same pitcher. One second you're on top, the next it's as good as all over. It is a story every pitcher in the major leagues knows by heart.

You try to tell yourself it was a freaky kind of thing. You try to tell yourself it can't happen to you. You try to tell yourself you'd be just that hundredth of a second quicker.

You tell yourself that if you're afraid, then there's no way you should be out there.

A Taste of Honey

It wasn't so much that we lost the pennant
but that we learned what it takes to win one

NICE GUY. NO HOPE.

If ever the spike fit, and it is one of the cruellest and most commonly applied cuts at every level of this game, it was on Kenny Schrom.

Manager Bobby Mattick told him as much one afternoon in March '81 as they sat on the bench and watched Jim Clancy work his way out of a jam in spring training. "Son," Schrom remembers the boss saying after Clancy walked a guy, "I'd really like to put you in this game, but we're trying to win it."

Schrom was dealt to Toronto in June '80, the player to be named later in a deal the week before that sent Dave Lemanczyk to the California Angels. He went straight to the farm club in Syracuse and, save for a couple of whistle stops with the big club, he spent the next two seasons there. The club cut him loose with a month left in the '82 season.

Three months later, as I sipped my morning coffee and poked through *The Sporting News*, I spotted a paragraph about him signing a Triple A contract with Minnesota. Some guys don't know when to give up.

He comes back from Toledo to pitch 200 innings for the Twins in '83, puts together a dandy 15–8 record (3.71 ERA) and on three occasions (4–3 at Toronto, 5–2 and 6–2 at Minneapolis) his victim is the Mr. Nice Guy who wished him so well that December morning. The irony that I finished 17–12 (3.04 ERA), three wins short of the magic twenty, was not lost on me.

Not for a moment, however, did I wonder what Mattick was thinking the day he whispered sweet nothings into Schrom's ear. The same oldtimer, after all, saw the makings of a pitcher in a certain college outfielder who should need no introduction.

In a way, it reminds me of our third basemen, Rance Mulliniks and Garth Iorg, and their struggles to achieve a sense (that's all it ever is) of belonging in the majors.

After three tries at the brass ring with the California Angels, Mulliniks was traded with Willie Aikens to the K.C. Royals. Some break. Just beat out George Brett, U.L. Washington or Frank White for a job on the left side of the infield. For two seasons, he warmed the bench until, just as camp broke in the spring of '82, he was dealt to Toronto for pitcher Phil Huffman. At twenty-six, playing more than one hundred games in the majors for the first time, he hit .244 with twenty-five doubles, then .275 (35 doubles) in '83, .324 in '84 and .295 (10 HRs) in '85.

Same thing, more or less, for Iorg, one of the three names on the roster that were at that first spring camp in '77. By the time he was twenty-five, he had played nineteen games in the majors. Over the next six seasons, his batting averages were .248, .242, .285, .275 and, after an unlikely .227 in '84, he led the team at .313 (twenty-two doubles) in '85.

I have an image of them, parked on stools a few stalls apart, newspaper guys gathered 'round, in the visitors' clubhouse at Fenway Park an hour before we opened the '83 season against the Boston Red Sox. Both of them were talking about our chances in the AL East and, for the first time, people were listening.

We won the game 7–1, Mulliniks backing his brave talk with a two-run homer in the second. Dennis Eckersley ran a pitch off his rump next time up and umpire Larry Barnett warned that any more "purpose" pitches would bring ejections. I nicked Big Jim Rice with two out in the fifth, the benches emptied and Red Sox manager Ralph Houk flipped when I wasn't tossed. Barnett doubted I would risk a shutout when I was only one out short of the five innings I needed to qualify for the win. He was right.

My next two decisions, a win and a loss against the New York Yankees, introduced me to a couple of faces that would become familiar over the next few seasons. Rookie Don Mattingly, jumping all over an errant slider, doubled for two runs in the seventh to ice a 3–0 loss. I squeaked by 6–5 the next week after we roughed up Doyle Alexander, an oldtimer supposed to be down and out, for seven hits in two innings. No, now that you mention it, I never would have guessed he would become the toast of Toronto one dank October afternoon a couple of years later. And yes, shades of Kenny Schrom, it says that being beaten does not mean being defeated.

As May dawned, I was 3–2 (1.58 ERA), the club's pitcher-of-the-month for April and thinking, with reasonable luck, I might crack the charmed circle of twenty-game winners. The month of May, maybe my best in the majors, convinced me this was the year. I was named American League pitcher of the month, rightfully so, for five victories (two shutouts), 57⅓ innings pitched, 35 hits, 11 earned runs and a 1.73 ERA.

We buried the White Sox 8–0 to start the month and mowed down K.C. 6–1 on ten strikeouts. As I warmed up for the ninth against the Royals, the crowd stood as one to applaud and did not sit down until Jesse Barfield, 4-for-4 with three RBIs, ended the game by throwing out a runner at the plate. As I walked off the mound, considering the things I had said in seasons past, I was grateful these people did not hold grudges.

The White Sox took me to ten innings back in Chicago, but we won it 3–1 on three singles and a sacrifice fly. The play of the month, which is not to suggest it was a fielding gem, sent it into extra innings. Ron Kittle swatted a one-hopper that glanced off my glove toward Willie Upshaw at first. I thought we might collide, so I chose to kick it. Right into Upshaw's glove. He flipped to me at first and we were out of the inning. Tinker to Evers to Chance it ain't, but they would have been proud. I could do no wrong.

We won 2–1 in eleven innings at Milwaukee when the Brewers stranded a dozen runners. The Orioles, 6–0 losers back in Toronto, provided me with another inning-long standing ovation. My record for the season was 8–2 (1.04 ERA); for the month, 5–0 (0.58 ERA). I was wondering if it was too good to last.

The Red Sox hammered us 7–2, ripping me for five earned runs in three innings. I had tried to be too fine with my pitches and, behind in the counts, let the fat stuff hang over the plate. I had a lock on my sixth win of the month in Detroit, a shutout into the ninth, but I loaded the bases on a walk and a pair of hits. Lance Parrish doubled off reliever Randy Moffitt and Rick Leach singled off Joey McLaughlin to tie it. We won 6–4 in the tenth on Alfredo Griffin's double, singles by Damaso Garcia and Buck Martinez.

With a 6–2 win over Oakland, I was the first in the majors to win nine, but my luck was about to run thin. Ernie Whitt hit a two-run homer at Anaheim to give us a 3–2 lead (and me a chance at number ten) over the California Angels heading into the ninth. Rod Carew slapped a single to left off Joey McLaughlin to tie it, but we won 6–5 in the fifteenth.

After an 8-2 start, I won my second in six outings with a 6-3 win over the Brewers, then lost the first two to Schrom within a week to close out a dreadful month of June (2-3, 4.46 ERA).

Almost as much as the All-Star Game in Chicago, I looked forward to battling Rick Honeycutt of the Texas Rangers a couple of days afterwards. Comparing his 11-4 record (1.52 ERA) and my 10-7 (2.54 ERA), there had been support for him to start the All-Star Game. We rattled him for three home runs, one more than he had given up all season, and the 6-4 victory put me at 11-7.

For a long time, it was my last hurrah.

I lost three in a row, a 14-8 blowout to K.C., 7-4 to Chicago and 3-1 to New York before, after nearly a month of waiting, I won my twelfth with an 8-0 wipeout of the Yankees.

What made it truly frustrating was the blister that had developed on my index finger in mid-July, limiting the use of my slider. Since early in June, I had gone to the mound fifteen times and had won but three decisions. We had been in a pennant race since the middle of May and, as the so-called ace of the staff, I felt badly about my contribution during the most critical stage of the franchise's existence.

After a 4-3 victory over the Brewers put me at 13-10, Big Jim Rice, who had been waiting since Opening Day, got his revenge by hitting a wind-blown home run with the bases loaded in Boston for a 5-2 victory.

Anyone who follows the team closely knows the season and our first real pennant threat went down the drain in Baltimore the last week of August. Luis Leal won the opener of the three-game series 9-3 to leave us 1½ games out of first. We were up 3-1 in the ninth the next night, with two outs left, but we lost it 7-4 in ten. I left after nine scoreless innings the next night and was as happy as if I had won it when Barry Bonnell homered in the tenth to give us a 1-0 lead. With one out in the Orioles' tenth, Joe Nolan and Al Bumbry singled off Roy Lee Jackson. Then Dan Ford doubled into center field, an eyelash past Lloyd Moseby's glove, and it was all over.

The *coup de grâce* was delivered in Detroit when we lost two of three and fell five games off the pace.

As much as I hate to admit it, we were not the team we were a couple of months earlier. A pennant chase had taken twenty-five young guys, from backgrounds that ranged from dirt poor to filthy rich, and made them one. Now it was over and the spirit of the clubhouse reflected it.

For a night game, the rule is that a player must show up in the clubhouse at 5.15 p.m., an hour earlier if he wants injury treatment from trainers Ken Carson or Tommy Craig. In the thick of it, guys couldn't wait to get to the ballpark and there was never any problem getting a foursome together for a Hearts game at two o'clock. Now, if it weren't for coach John Sullivan, Jim Acker would have had to play solitaire.

My record improved to 14–11 my first outing in September, but it took ten innings and a three-run homer by Ernie Whitt off the top of the fence in centre field. Next time out, against the Oakland A's, I had no one to blame but myself for blowing leads of 2–0 and 5–4 but we scrambled back to win it 7–5. How they stuck with me for seven innings is a mystery. A shrink might find some explanation for it, but the beard I had been growing for six weeks came off in the showers that day.

Kenny Schrom and the Twins trimmed me for the last time that season, but I bounced back in a 7–3 victory over the Mariners to improve to 16–12. Willie Upshaw drove in his 100th and 101st runs and, since I logged my 269th inning pitched, I needed only six more to cash in a $50,000 bonus.

When the team is out of it, when there are no individual awards left to the individual, you tend to keep score at the bank. I had earned $10,000 that year for pitching 225 and another $15,000 for reaching 250. There was a lot of newspaper talk about the $50,000 the day of my final outing.

I made it easy for the scribes with a called third strike against the Twins' Gary Ward to end the sixth, en route to a three-hit, 8–0 victory.

A couple of afternoons later, it was all over for '83, but there wasn't one of us that day who didn't think we could have been, should have been, counting on some playoff loot.

Still, the spirit Mulliniks and Iorg had exemplified that day we opened in Boston prevailed as we packed for home. We had not lost a pennant, we felt, so much as we learned what it took to win one.

The Dark Side

It took Dennis Lamp a season in hell to prove it
but he was the tonic for an ailing bullpen

I DON'T KNOW if I am all alone in this regard or if it happens this way with a lot of people, but the most curious images come to mind when I try to remember a given year of my life in baseball.

It ought to be the big stuff, like the first pitch of an All-Star Game or the play that dropped my earned run average to second best in the league, but what I recall instead are the "moments in between."

The 1984 season, for example.

All sorts of thoughts ought to occur to me, aided by visions of Sparky Anderson and a skewer of Tigers roasting over a pit of coals, but the one that crowds all of them out is of a sad-faced clown, his head in his hands, about as close to tears as I can stand to see a grown man get.

Dennis Lamp.

It happened one Sunday afternoon in Boston, where all manner of foul things can befall an honest workman, and it happened after the Red Sox (and that bloody wall everybody thinks is so quaint) beat us 5–3 in ten innings.

127

I have to take some of the blame.

We were ahead 3–0 with two out and the bases loaded in the bottom of the ninth on a pair of singles and, dammit, a walk. Up comes pinch-hitter Reid Nichols, a .226 hitter that season. He bloops a swell 1–2 pitch off that wall in left to cash in all the three runs. Any other ballpark, so help me, and George Bell would have had it in his hip pocket.

Had the good folks of New England been able to read my lips at that moment, or my thoughts when manager Bobby Cox sent me to inspect the clubhouse bathing facilities a moment later, I am certain I would have joined the long and celebrated list of things banned in Boston. A sure 3–0 victory in my grasp, a neat-and-tidy four-hitter all but in the books, and it had slipped away. Worse for me, I now had only one win to show for my last five starts. I was ready to eat nails, guzzle gunpowder, shoot first and explain it all later.

Dammit, I was mad.

I cursed The Wall. I cursed Mike Easler, Bill Buckner and their two puny singles in the ninth. I cursed myself and the umpire for the walk we gave up to load the bases. I cursed George Bell for not scaling the Green Monster to make a circus catch of Nichols' pop fly. And, bad sign, I was looking for the clubhouse boy to curse him for not having the common decency to stock my brand of soap.

All this, mind you, on a Sunday.

Now, a few minutes after Tony Armas had hit the two-run homer that made losers of us all in the tenth inning, I happened to look up and see Lamp with his head down a few lockers away.

We had signed him the previous January, the club's second choice for a short reliever after the San Diego Padres had won the bidding for Rich Gossage. Right or wrong, we expected Lamp to give us what we thought the Goose would have given us. It had not worked out that way. Not at all. The year before, as the "lock-up" man for the Chicago White

Sox during the second half of their runaway in the West Division, Lamp had reeled off most of his fifteen saves. As a free agent, he got a five-year deal in the neighborhood of $2.5 million and, having been starved for a quality stopper, the fans expected him to earn it in one season. It had been too much to ask, particularly from a guy whose history was in long relief or as a starter.

In Baltimore, a month before Boston, he got the call in the seventh inning after I put a 3–0 lead in jeopardy by loading the bases with one out. Cal Ripken drilled a single for two runs. Eddie Murray smacked a base hit to tie the game. We won it, fortunately, on Barry Bonnell's homer in the tenth.

In Cleveland, a couple of months after Boston, Lamp inherited a 5–2 lead from me after eight innings. With the bases full on two singles and a walk, Brett Butler rolled a single down the first-base line for one run. Another Indian came home on a fielder's choice. As if to taunt him, Mike Hargrove struck out and Andre Thornton got behind 1–2 to put Lamp within a strike of survival. Smack! Line drive to right-center, inches off the tip of Lloyd Moseby's glove, and two runs score. Game over.

As badly as I felt after each of these setbacks—winning them, as I ought to have, would have given me a record of 19–8—I honestly felt worse for Lamp. He was better by far than the grim line of numbers that appeared beside his name each day in the public prints. He proved it, too, the next season. From 8–8 (4.55 ERA) as a short reliever in '84 to 11–0 (3.32) in long relief in '85 makes it obvious that he was the right man who, for a time, happened to be in the wrong place.

What I liked most about him, in spite of his awful jokes and his goofy impersonations of Joe Frazier and Muhammad Ali, was his sunny disposition under all that pressure. Save for that one time in Boston, when it seemed to be closing in on him, I never saw him abandon his belief that it would come out right in the end.

Rarely will I console a teammate after his honest efforts have cost us a game and there are some, I admit, who think "my magnanimity lacking" (their words, not mine, whatever they mean) in such situations. I know that when it is me at fault, which can be often enough in the course of a season of thirty-five starts, I am all too aware of what went wrong. In these situations, a little positive reinforcement from a teammate goes a long way. I am not alone in this line of thinking. Win a hundred games in a season, which will put any team within arm's length of the World Series, and it still leaves sixty-two losses to be pinned on somebody. This could lead to a lot of sappy talk. Lose, I believe, and you should feel badly.

With Lamp, at least that gray Sunday afternoon in Boston, I felt an exception was in order. I wandered over, spread my arm across his shoulder and whispered in his ear. "What the hell," I said, "you could have taken it to fifteen innings. At least this way, we don't miss the dinner flight to Milwaukee." He looked up, lit that whacko smile of his and suggested, perhaps quite rightly, that I attempt the physically impossible.

Oh, well . . .

The way events were unfolding in Detroit that season, Lamp would have had to walk on water to make a real difference in the East Division race. Sparky's Boys were off to a 35–5 start and, even though we were making a shambles of our own club records, it had become a game of follow the leader.

As encouraging as it was frustrating for me was the fact I was off to a flying start, but that the team seemed to be spinning its wheels in its chase of the Tigers. Here it was, the beginning of June, and we were 5½ games out of first place. What was shocking was that my 2–1 victory over the White Sox, making me 7–1 at the end of May, made it thirteen out of the last fifteen for us and our nineteenth win of the month.

About all it proved to me was that spring training, at least for me, is a couple of weeks too long. That's how much I missed after twisting my ankle about six weeks before the season began. Maybe some players need six weeks but, personally, I think it's for the sportswriters. Sweating out nine innings in a hot press box, especially with all those cold beers and hot dogs back at the Labatt's hospitality center, takes discipline. Sometimes, I wonder where they find the stamina.

Though you try your best not to get too far ahead of yourself, we had an idea even then that the entire season might be shaped by a four-game series with the Tigers in June.

Never was I more ready.

In my wake were a string of victims. The California Angels crashed 3–1, with seven strikeouts in as many innings, aided by the first of Lloyd Moseby's eighteen home runs. Dave Collins stroked three hits and swiped two bases in a 7–1 victory over Jim Palmer and the Baltimore Orioles in which I gave up five hits over eight innings. The Mariners went under 8–5, on eight hits over 7⅓ innings. The Royals, without George Brett (injury) and Willie Wilson (suspension), folded 6–0 in K.C., but took me into the tenth inning at home before we pulled out a 4–3 squeaker.

I liked what I saw in myself that day my record went to 5–0 to match a club mark for a season start. After Darryl Motley crushed a hanging slider for a three-run homer in the second inning, not one Royal got as far as third base the rest of the way. Though we rattled five pitchers for fifteen hits, it took Alfredo Griffin's surprise bunt single with two out in the tenth to win it.

After being taken off the hook for a 1–0 loss in Minnesota, a game we tied in the ninth and won 5–2 in ten innings, I should have figured my luck was about to thin out.

My 3–0 loss to the Chicago White Sox was curious for at least a couple of reasons, the lesser being the first time since the previous August we had been shut out at home. The other was that, for the first time since the Washington Senators planted one Joe Kuhel there for a game in 1937, the White Sox had a left-hander (Mike Squires) playing at third base. As a student of the game, this curiosity and the defensive possibilities it presents intrigued me. Late in a close game, when a third baseman hugs the line to prevent a double into the corner, it might make sense to deploy a left-hander there. His glove hand closest to the line, he might be able to field such a smash a little more cleanly. To compensate for what he gives up to his left side, he could station himself a little further off the line. Earlier in the game, I would think, the disadvantages of having to backhand a lot of grounders and make the awkward pivots to throw would outweigh the benefits. (He would also get a lot of practice fielding bunts.) Squires played about a dozen games at third that year and, from what I hear, did a fair job. Certainly, for a team I have beaten twelve times in fifteen meetings, he didn't hurt them that day.

After polishing off the Indians 5–1 on a three-hitter over eight innings and slipping past the White Sox 2–1 (four hits, 8⅓ innings), I was eager to see if the Tigers were as ferocious as their start suggested.

For a while there that Monday night, up until the final out of the seventh inning to be precise, I believed the best team was winning 3–0. That's when Howard Johnson stepped up, with two men on base (Chet Lemon, hit by a pitch; Dave Bergman, single to right) and wrapped a fastball around the foul pole in right for three runs to tie it.

It was the only time in his four seasons as manager that Coxie came anywhere close to taking a strip off me in public. "When you've got a three-run lead in the seventh inning, you can't blow it," he told the writers afterwards. "Hit a guy and then give a guy a slow curve, that's no way to start an inning." The belt-high fastball to HoJo wasn't so bright, either, but I was in no mood for confessions.

Three innings later, after battling Roy Lee Jackson for a dozen pitches, Bergman killed us off with a three-run homer in the tenth.

We won the next two and lost on getaway day for a split of the series, but looking back, I have to say our best chance went down the tubes that week. Any doubt was erased when we lost four in a row at Yankee Stadium, my contribution a 2–1 loss to Ron Guidry. Steve Kemp's double to the wall in right-center scored Dave Winfield with the winner in the ninth inning. At least half-a-dozen times that game, we had runners in scoring position with less than two out.

We trounced the Tigers 12–3 and 7–3 back in Toronto that week—my record going to 8–2 with the second victory— to prove to ourselves that we belonged with them. In seven head-to-head games that June, we outscored them 43–29, out-hit them 77–60 and out-homered them 10–4. It's good for morale, I suppose, which pays for the morning paper in most towns if you can scrape up twenty-five cents to go with it.

There was no way, it became all too apparent, we were going to pin a tail on the Tigers. When we went on a rip, they went on a tear. When they skidded, we came to a stop. With first place gone, save for the miracle that was not going to happen, personal pride can bring out the best in some players.

Rick Leach, three times a Rose Bowl quarterback and considered a cinch to star in baseball when he graduated from the University of Michigan, had been dumped that spring after three so-so seasons with the Tigers. Instead of walking away, as many might have done, he signed with our farm club in Syracuse. He came back up a couple of months later, the reason obvious one July night when he made a play to beat the California Angels. On the front end of an apparent double play, he made a bone-crunching block at second to keep an inning alive. "Foul play," Angels manager John McNamara beefed. "Country hardball," Coxie responded. In similar circumstances, I have seen lots of guys pull up, but Leach's effort led to a three-run inning and a 6–3 win. In the boxscore the next morning, it was just one of twenty-four outs we made that night.

All summer, Dave Collins had been doing similar stuff. The fourth outfielder coming out of spring training, his play forced Coxie to use him in 125 games that season, hitting .308 and stealing 60 bases. In one of those outings, a 2–1 win over Oakland that boosted my record to 10–3, he swatted an opposite-field single in the ninth that landed maybe a foot inside the line. In September, with nothing but the pride of second place at stake, he engineered a 6–4 victory over the Brewers (that made me 15–7) by scoring three runs, driving in two (his eleventh game-winning RBI) and stealing his fifty-sixth base.

Performances like these prevented me from losing my grip on the eight days when I ended up a loser. For some curious reason, for which I long ago stopped searching, the club seemed to produce fewer runs when I was pitching.

In two of those eight losses, 5–4 to the Royals and 14–6 to the Red Sox—I left in the six-run fifth, down 8–4—I agree they provided enough support. In the six others, the average was about 1½ runs. The rule, I admit, is that all one needs to do is to hold the opponent to one less run. Still, although these squeakers made me a better pitcher, my queasy stomach would have appreciated a few more blowouts.

For three weeks around that time, I hit a dry spell, no decisions in four starts, but I knew better than to think the Indians would end the drought. Score 1–1 in the ninth, two out and a man on, Jerry Willard hits a two-run homer.

Rance Mulliniks, as he often does, put it right with a 3-for-3 (home run, double) day at the plate to account for our runs in a 2–1 win over the Minnesota Twins during which I struck out eleven and walked one.

A 6–2 loss to the Yankees a couple of weeks later served to confirm mathematically what we had known for weeks.

The Tigers would represent the East in the playoffs. Our struggle now, complicated by the Orioles' rush to respectability, was to hang on to second place. The Tigers, as if to deprive us, dropped me 2–1 on Ruppert Jones's homer in the fourth and his spectacular catch of Cliff Johnson's bid for a homer in the eighth.

Although we clung to second place, which I considered a worthy accomplishment, I lost the ERA title in my second-last outing of the season to Mike Boddicker of the Orioles (2.83 to 2.79) in that 14–6 blowout by the Red Sox.

There was one brutal call by the official scorer, which I figure cost me a couple of earned runs and the title, but what's the sense of complaining?

I was mad about it all winter, I confess, but I think it gave me a little extra incentive to get even the next summer.

Wrong Numbers

With luck like I had in '85, I have to wonder
if somebody up there doesn't like me

PERSONALLY (HINT, HINT) I can think of people I would rather have receive it, but I can make no quarrel with the selection of Bret Saberhagen of the Kansas City Royals as the '85 winner of the Cy Young Award.

His 2.78 earned run average was a shade higher than the 2.48 posted by my favorite candidate and most of his pitching was done in the West Division, but his 20–6 record was much better than the numbers (14–13) I put on the board. What he did in the World Series, winning twice and allowing only one run in eighteen innings to capture MVP honors, only confirmed that the baseball writers made the right choice when they cast their votes.

Dammit.

Saberhagen had the season I wanted to have. Deserved to have. Should have had. If that sounds arrogant, hold the ice cream when you serve me my hot humble pie.

Double dammit.

I know that figures lie, that liars figure and that baseball

137

is a breeding ground for both activities. Just the same, the statistical evidence suggests to me that a big black cloud took up permanent residence over the Great Lakes last season and slipped into Toronto on days when I was pitching. Must have sent word to its cousins all over the States, too, considering the way its evil influence dogged me on my travels throughout the American League.

It might sound like sour grapes to some—and no one hates a whiner more than I do—but the statistical story that appeared in the *1986 Elias Baseball Analyst* stumps me even now after a new season has begun and all those shining goals wait impatiently to be achieved. What follows is an excerpt from what Seymour Siwoff, president of the Elias Sports Bureau, wrote in pinpointing three reasons for my uninspiring won-lost record:

> First, lack of batting support: Toronto gave Stieb slightly fewer runs to work with than their average, scoring 4.44 runs a game in Stieb's thirty-six starts, 4.79 for their other starting pitchers; they scored two or fewer runs for Stieb nine times.
>
> Second, lack of fielding support: Errors led to sixteen unearned runs charged to Stieb; only six American League pitchers allowed more. Twenty-seven per cent of Toronto's unearned runs were charged to Stieb, who accounted for only eighteen per cent of their innings pitched.
>
> Third, and most damning, lack of relief support: No fewer than six times, relievers blew leads that Stieb had delivered to them.

Nor was it something that escaped the fans.

In a letter to columnist John Robertson of the Toronto *Sun*, reader Vince Cammisuli compared my efforts with those of Saberhagen.

His argument, and it will be around as long as grown men play this little boys' game, is that earned run average is the most accurate barometer of a pitcher's worth. Others contend that winning the game is what matters, that so long as a pitcher comes out one run ahead, 10–9 or 6–5 or 1–0, what remains serves only to fill the pauses over a few beers after the game. If a pitcher is consistent, as when he wins twenty games a season, then who's to say he isn't as good or better than the man with a lower earned run average?

What makes the Stieb–Saberhagen equation the stuff of which such arguments are made is that I pitched 29⅔ more innings (265 to 235⅓) and still gave up two fewer earned runs, one for every eleven outs compared with one every 9.4 outs. In twelve of my thirty-six starts, I allowed just twenty-one earned runs, for a 2.02 ERA, but came away with six losses and six no-decisions. If the club had scored enough runs to win half of them, I would have had my twenty victories. In twenty-seven starts, I gave up two earned runs or less—no earned runs seven times, one earned run nine times, two earned runs eleven times—but wound up 13–7 with seven no-decisions. In the eleven games where I gave up two runs, the club scored enough runs to win only three.

I am proud that my ERA was the best in the league, but baseball is first a team game, so I am committed to saying I would have been happier by far winning twenty and settling for less success as an individual. In any case, if you argue the merits of either position long enough, you might end up doing your pitching in a rubber room.

Any pitcher can tell you about wrapping one up, handing it over to the bullpen to tie the ribbon and winding up going home from the party with empty hands. It came on my second start of the season, with a 7–2 lead over the Baltimore Orioles that became an 8–7 loss, a 6–0 shutout in Minneapolis a month later that became a 7–6 loss, and in August against the Twins again, a 5–2 lead in the eighth that became a 6–5 setback in ten with the help of four errors.

It never fails. The moment I think I have seen it all, this game pops up to remind me that I haven't. This time, though not for the first time, it happened one night in Milwaukee when we were doing our best imitation of the June swoon.

We're behind 2–1 going into the eighth inning, the lead run courtesy of a sloppy slider that second baseman Jim Gantner drilled out of the park in the fifth. Len Matuszek, whom we later traded to the L.A. Dodgers for Al Oliver, singled to put the tying run on base with two out in the eighth. Rookie Lou Thornton, in a rare excursion off the bench, drilled a shot to right field that was good for three bases. Not a triple, mind you. On an appeal play, ump Terry Cooney called him out for failing to touch first base. No hit, no run, no tie.

About six weeks earlier, the California Angels snapped a seven-game winning streak for the team with a 3–2 win over me after going into the final inning down 2–1. Ruppert Jones singled, Reggie walked, Rob Wilfong nubbed a single off the end of his bat to tie it. Jim Acker got Jerry Narron for the second out, but pinch-hitter Juan Beniquez singled, off the fists, for the game. Aaaarrrgh!

There were teams, too, that seemed to have our number when I was out there.

Willie Wilson's windblown fly ball to left field late in the seventh inning cost me a 2–1 loss to Bud Black on Opening Day in K.C. The next week in Toronto, Charlie Leibrandt beat me 2–0 on homers by Steve Balboni (hanging slider) and Darryl Motley (off-speed fastball). Later in the season at K.C., a pitcher's ballpark, I was looking for my first win in a couple of weeks. Balboni's homer, the first I had given up in eight career starts (sixty-one innings) at Royals Stadium, buried me 4–2.

The Indians, a team that finished nearly forty games behind us in the East Division, played like pennant-winners the three times I faced them.

Early in June, we're leading 4–2 in the opener of a doubleheader when Jerry Willard comes to the plate in the ninth with one out and the bases loaded. The year before, he beat me with a homer in the last inning, so this time I was determined to do better. And I did. He doubled. For three runs. We lost 5–4. With me, at least, the Indians were consistent. A couple of months later, they won 5–3, their second victory in nine games against us, the second time they had scored as many as five runs against us and, yes, the second time I was the victim. It evened out (a little) a couple of weeks later with a 3–2 squeaker in Toronto on Labor Day. What a breeze that was is detailed elsewhere in this book.

Lest this recitation create the impression that I was perfection personified, let me hasten to assure there were times when, in danger of going down in flames, I splashed gasoline on the fire.

What might be my worst inning as a pro occurred late in July, repayment for a 10–1 drubbing of the Oakland A's that ruined the homecoming of Alfredo Griffin and Dave Collins. In eight innings of a 5–1 loss, I gave up eleven hits, one short of my career high. Seven of them, for four runs, were in the second inning and included a triple by Griffin that fell between outfielders who lost the ball in the glare of the screen behind home plate.

There were times, too, when the bullpen saved me from hopping from the frying pan into the fire.

Late in April against the Rangers at Texas, Coxie decided not to bring me back after a 104-minute rain delay. It had nothing to do, he fibbed, with the three runs and four hits I had given up in a couple of innings. We won 9–8 in the tenth, but it took a two-run homer by Willie Aikens—his last at-bat with the club—to give us the chance. The Rangers provided me with my first success of the season, a 4–2 victory in which I worked seven sloppy innings. Lavelle and Acker bailed me out of a bases-loaded situation with a sac fly and a groundout.

It was a season, for all my lamentations about hard luck, that also provided me with some of the finest moments of my career.

As I expect they will be for seasons to come, the Detroit Tigers were a challenge that brought out the best in me. Everybody knows beating them is as simple as keeping Lou Whitaker and Al Trammell off the bases and Kirk Gibson, Lance Parrish and Darrell Evans inside the park. I did it, too, the first two times we met, allowing five hits in fifteen shutout innings, to win 9–2 in Toronto and 2–0 on a three-hitter before 48,000 fans in Tiger Stadium.

Modest though I try to be, I have to say that last outing was an example of me at my best and that the assessment takes in more than getting the ball to the plate and past the hitters. In the third inning, with Chet Lemon and Tom Brookens on base, Whitaker went by the book and laid down a bunt. I pounced on it, but with 48,000 voices ringing in my ears, I couldn't hear anybody telling me to which base I should throw. Because he hit it fairly hard, I guessed we had a chance for Lemon at third. I was right and, on that blind decision, a ballgame turned. I held them to a pair of singles the rest of the way. The shutout pared my ERA to 1.95 and my opponents' batting average for the season to .188. I will settle for those numbers any time.

Later in the season, as we battled to clinch the pennant, the Tigers' Darrell Evans put my name in the record books when he poked his fortieth home run of the season to become the first player to hit that many in both the National and American Leagues.

The Yankees, too, wrote a number of memorable entries for the scrapbooks gathering dust in my closet.

Though I had been lifted after walking Willie Randolph with one out in the ninth in a game in June, Rance Mulliniks homered in the tenth for a 3–2 victory that proved to me the club had learned to win the close ones. We were down 2–0 after seven, but scratched out runs in the final two innings to give Rance a chance. Earlier in the game, Jesse Barfield was knocked out diving for Rickey Henderson's sinking liner, which went for a triple. Blood streaming from his mouth, he refused to be taken out of the game. What a gamer.

Same score the following month in Toronto, but we needed a break to win it in the tenth. With Lloyd Moseby and Willie Upshaw on base, George Bell hit a slow roller to Mike Pagliarulo. The Yankees third baseman lunged to tag Moseby and, missing, threw off-balance to first. The ball got away and Moseby romped home for the 3–2 win.

With breaks like these, I guess I should have expected things to go wrong when we showed up at Yankee Stadium in September for the four-game series that decided the division race. I was at my best (two hits) and worst (five walks) but held a 4–1 lead heading into the seventh inning. With one out, I gave Willie Randolph the sixth pass, but figured I had dodged the bullet again when Bobby Meacham slapped a two-hopper to Tony Fernandez near second base. As Tony moved toward second, to start the double play to end the inning, Damaso Garcia peeled off. Fernandez flipped the ball and, in my dreams for the rest of my days, I will see it kick up the dirt and trickle away. The floodgates opened for a six-run inning and, eventually, a 7–5 loss. Had he been a step closer or a step further away when he fielded the ball, Fernandez told me later, there would not have been the hesitation on what play to make. I told him the next day that he had won any number of games for the club and would be winning them for seasons to come. I meant it then. I mean it now.

As much as I say that fisticuffs is an activity best suited for the ring, I would be fibbing if I said our battle with the Red Sox that June was anything but memorable. Since the events preceding George Bell's drop-kick to pitcher Bruce Kison's solar plexus and pirouette left hook to catcher Rich Gedman's mandible got more airplay than the afternoon soaps,

I see no need here to dredge up the gory details. What I never will forget, however, is the picture of Ernie Whitt rounding first base, right arm thrust high, as his grand-slam homer off Kison cleared the fence. For all the punches thrown a couple of innings earlier, this was the one that did the most damage.

That it was Whitt who did it, one of the three players left from that first spring camp in '77, did my heart good.

Somehow, as I saw him rounding the bases and shouting his defiance at Kison, I knew we had arrived as a club.

We had come a long way.

Work Ethic

When you've got a lot, they want a lot;
when you've got a little, they want it all

THE SUN IS AS HIGH as a pop fly in a sky far too blue, far too bland for an outfielder's eyes, but there are clumps of cloud in the distance—huge, lazy swirls of them over Lake Ontario—that will draw the heat by the time the game begins.

Labor Day. Great day for a ballgame. Where's Ernie Banks? Let's play two. Indian summer is here early and winter can't be far behind.

The stands are filled with kids, on an afternoon's respite from the three-week summer fair the city of Toronto holds on the Canadian National Exhibition grounds where our ballpark stands. They are in full cry as they prepare for the passing of sentence tomorrow that will commit them to their books and schoolrooms for another year.

If they were here looking for a lesson in the art of great pitching, they would have been better off by far had they never left the game booths along the midway outside. There, for half a dollar, the man takes a kewpie doll home if he can toss the strike that knocks three milk bottles off a shelf. Pressure. That's what pitching is all about.

145

The way I was confusing them that afternoon, they couldn't have been learning much about this glorious art form by watching me. I won it 3–2, with help from the bullpen, and I was lucky.

The Indians greeted me with three singles to center field in the first inning and, on a pickoff attempt at second base, I threw the ball into center field. E-1. Lovely. So I struck out the side. Damage: one run. With a fistful of half-dollars, I might do all right myself on the midway.

I loaded the bases the next inning and escaped, by the skin of a baseball, with no damage. I walked the leadoff man in the third and picked him off first base. Then, with two out, Brett Butler got a break when an infielder lost a soft liner in the glare off the screen behind the plate. He stole a base and came home on a single. Cheap run, but they all count.

Devastated I was not. Mad, really mad, I was. At myself. And with good reason. I'm sure you're aware of my little performance when I get upset. Slam the resin bag. Stomp around the mound. Yank the bill of my cap. Glare at the batter. Grind my teeth. And, yes, curse a blue streak any schoolkid could decipher with the help of a TV cameraman and his zoom lens.

I know this might be difficult to believe but, off the field, my language is such that it would be and has been quite acceptable at a Sunday church social. On the field, at times when all that I am is in jeopardy, I've spewed curses that would make a coven of witches quail.

My skirmishes with the English language are not something that makes me particularly proud but, considering the circumstances, I don't think I'm all that different from the carpenter who has just nailed his thumb to the crossbeam. I'm sorry, but not as sorry as I am for what caused me to lose my temper.

I do what it takes to drive me to win. Anger is a tool I

employ on the job, just like a plumber uses a monkey-wrench. Surprising though it might be to those who have paid for home repairs lately, I make more per hour than he does, but then again he doesn't have 30,000 customers pulling his chain when he makes a mistake. It can make you tense.

It's not the type of behavior I would like to see on the sandlot, where the object of the game is to see how much fun a kid can have. Nor am I all that pleased when, in the replays on the tube later that night, I see how the demons took hold. I am aware that I help set an example. At this level of the game there is so much at stake that, it often becomes more than the game it was intended to be.

Sure, there are guys so cool out there you'd think they were on a Sunday stroll. Some people call it poise. When I hear that word, I cringe. Maybe they're good at bottling it up and, maybe they don't show any emotion because they don't care. Win or lose, they're getting their six figures, so why sweat it? It's not just another day on the job for me. This is my three hours to do what I can do best. When it is over, I have to wait four days for another chance and sometimes, as it was one awful night last October, an entire winter.

Competitive? Make your first two pitches strikes and the conventional wisdom is to waste the third one, the theory being that, with the hitter this deep in a hole, he tends to become less selective. It makes sense, too, but it goes against the grain. Not only is it another pitch on my arm, but it is contrary to the first rule of pitching, which is to throw strikes. I'll "waste one" on occasion, but in the back of my mind, I want it close enough so that it might catch a corner of the plate.

You would think, too, that big guns like Dave Winfield, Eddie Murray, Reggie Jackson et al. would be enough of a challenge for a "power pitcher" with the taste for blood. Know what bugs me most? Giving up a rookie's first hit in the major leagues. I can see him now, the lights flashing in his beady little eyes as he sets himself in the batter's box, looking for a story he can tell the grandchildren. Damned if it's going to be me.

Darryl Sconiers, called up from the minors to spell the great Rod Carew at first base for fifteen games late in the 1981 season, took it one step further when he added minor injury to the insult of ringing me up for his first hit in the majors. It was a smash past my ear and, proving the paw is quicker than the brain, I put my right hand in front of it. It caught me at the base of the thumb but X-rays at the hospital turned up no lasting damage. "A couple of inches the other way," manager Bobby Mattick told the newspapers, "and it would have killed him." If you ask me, it was my pride that hurt the most.

Emotional? I also plead guilty. Just tell me on thing. If I were taking your money to do a job, would you care that I didn't care if I wasn't giving it everything I had? I don't think you'll have to think too hard on that one. And if there was a lesson that day for the kids who saw me, it is that they might not have seen me at my best, but they saw me giving it my best. Promise that much to the manager—it's a rule by which you live or die with Jimy Williams and, before him, Bobby Cox and Bobby Mattick—and you just might never see the inside of his doghouse.

It took years to develop the mean streak I take to the mound—mind you, it stops short of doing anything that would put a career in jeopardy. The metamorphosis, if that's what it was, might have begun just as I was entering my teens and the family moved 500 miles from Yorba Linda up the California coast to San Jose, so my dad could get a better job.

Not that it could be helped, but there are doctors, rich ones, who will tell you that a move at this time of life, when a kid has cemented his first friendships, can be a wrenching experience. It was for me. Like most kids at that age, I was in the midst of an identity crisis. Who am I? What am I doing here? What will I be when I grow up? Is there anybody out there who likes me?

In the midst of all this confusion, my older brother Steve and I had to crack a new high school in San Jose. He was a catcher, a pretty good one, which he proved by winning the job, as a sophomore, on the Oak Grove High varsity team from a guy who was known and liked. It boosted my confidence to consider it a family feat. I was pretty much in search of everything. Friends. Being accepted. Making the freshman team. I did, too, but I had to switch from the infield, which I played all through Little League, to the outfield.

My fragile psyche wasn't helped any the next summer when, during the first practice game for the junior varsity team, I broke my ankle sliding into third base and was out for the season. It was one of the longest summers of my life. Because of it, I was assigned to the junior varsity team the next season, even though I knew I was good enough for the big club.

I gathered my courage, a trait only then in the budding stage, and put it to coach John Bessa. He must have wondered who this kid was, telling him there was no way he should be kept off the varsity squad even if he did miss the entire previous season. He gave me my chance, I won the job in left field and had a fair year. Even if I say so myself, I was sensational the next season (.417 batting average) and in my first year of junior college, they moved established guys around so I could play center field.

It took all of five years, but I had grown from boy to young man. Baseball was the forge that stoked my confidence and, with it, sharpened a fierce competitive edge.

There are times, I admit, when I let it get away from me. Glaring at my teammates when they make a mistake is bad. Bush league. I admit it. It's a thing I used to do early in my career in the majors and it is nothing in which I take any great pride.

What caused it, I have to say, is the change in roles I had to make when I was converted from an outfielder to a pitcher at the outset of my pro career. As an outfielder, as a hitter, what you did was what you did. No more. No less. You catch the ball. You throw the ball. You hit the ball. You run the bases. The job was finished. When you pitch, for the most part your success is in other hands. Once you let go of the ball, unless it is hit back at you, it's up to other people to make the play. Maybe if I had been a pitcher when I was a kid, maybe if I had more than nineteen starts (128 innings) in the minor leagues, I would have learned to cope more ably with that immutable law of the game.

And perhaps, to be honest, I ought to have been aware a lot earlier that I should be developing a little tighter grip on my emotional side. Maybe because he had a fair temper himself when he was a pitcher in the old days, it was something that came to the notice of John Oldham, my baseball coach in junior college. It happened, as always seems to be the case with me, in a most curious way.

Like me, right fielder Charlie Stauffer was a "red ass," so we made a pact at the beginning of the season to keep each other in line when our tempers got out of hand. We soon discovered two things: 1) There is great satisfaction in searching out major character flaws (like your own) in someone else; 2) If anything, it makes them worse. We rode each other so hard in one game that coach Oldham hauled us off the field and put us on the bench for the rest of the afternoon. Our experiment in constructive criticism was over.

This failing was a source of some embarrassment to me and a number of my teammates in the early stages of my career in the major leagues.

Alvis Woods, who pinch-hit a home run the day the team

played its first game in '77, was the victim one night in August of '81 in a game at Toronto against the Texas Rangers. It was the sixth inning and I had done myself no favors in giving up seven hits, including a home run, hitting two batters, walking three and throwing a wild pitch. There were two on when shortstop Mario Mendoza lifted a fly ball into left field. I don't know if he lost it in the lights, whether he misjudged the distance to the fence, or if he was afraid of going through it, but Woods pulled up. When it landed, at the base of the fence, I couldn't believe it. Two runs scored. All the way back to the mound from behind third base, where I had been covering, I glared at that spot. I flipped my glove in the air. I didn't even wait for coach Denis Menke, coming out of the dugout with the hook, to arrive at the mound. I handed the ball to Danny Ainge, who was trying to cool me out, and walked back to the dugout casting venomous looks toward left field.

As soon as I had entered the hallway leading to the clubhouse, I knew I was wrong.

Afterwards, in the dressing room, Woods confirmed my suspicions in no uncertain terms. I apologized, which is a hard thing for me to do even when I'm wrong, but I knew it was too late with too little after I had shown him up in front of the crowd.

Catcher Buck Martinez also showed remarkable restraint in the face of a tantrum in June of '83 during a game against the Chicago White Sox at Comiskey Park.

We were ahead 3-1 in the seventh inning, with Bull Luzinski at the plate and two runners on base. Even though I had gotten Luzinski out on sliders all day, Buck called for a low fastball, which The Bull generally devours. Against my better judgment, I threw it and Luzinski crushed it for a three-run homer. I threw up my hands, angry at Buck for calling the pitch and just as upset with myself for not throwing it as low and as inside as Buck had wanted.

The next day, outfielder Barry Bonnell told me Buck would be happy to accept any nominations to kick my smart ass from Chicago to Caracas. I did what I should have done the night before. I apologized for being such a jerk and showing him up in front of the crowd. I said I had been frustrated but that I had no right to blame him.

Al Widmar, our kindly pitching coach, has the perfect answer for a pitcher who doesn't agree with a catcher's signal: "Even donkeys can shake their heads."

I won't say that I am now without fault, but I think I have a much better grip on my competitive zeal. About time, too.

Still, I wouldn't want to become too passive. Cast out the devils, after all, and the angels just might go, too.

Mental Cruelty

You don't have to be crazy to play this game
but there are afternoons when it helps

THE NEXT BEST THING to playing and winning is playing and losing.

It's the kind of consoling thought that occurs to you—OK, the brand of bullfish I was trying to pitch myself one dreary Saturday afternoon in August '85—when life takes your best shots and splashes them all over the scoreboard in right field.

The Texas Rangers, the worst team in the second-best division of the best league in baseball, had stoned me for seven earned runs a couple of hours before and now, as the evening's shadows creep across the ceiling of the bedroom, scenes of the Saturday matinee shootout are crowding in on me again.

In every game there is a turning point and, for me in this one, it must have been the moment the ump said, "Play ball!" So help me, it was that kind of a day.

For instance . . .

Toby Harrah is in a slump, which is to say that he has not drawn a walk in six games, but he works me for his eighty-eighth of the season with one out in the seventh. Gino Petralli, a catcher we dealt to the Cleveland Indians the summer before, throws his bat at a pitchout (a pitchout!) and lofts a single over Tony Fernandez's glove into left-center. I get a break on Curtis Wilkerson's tap back to the mound and, with first base open, I am not about to be hurt again by Oddibe McDowell, who hit a homer a couple of innings back. I walk him so I can pitch to Wayne Tolleson.

Admittedly, nothing in this life is sure except death and double taxes but, after waving at two nasty sliders, I figure I have the guy eating out of my Wilson A-2000 fielder's glove. Then he cues the third one, the nastiest slider yet, a foot or two foul down the first base line, but it curls back and kicks off the bag for a base hit. What had been a 3–3 nail-biter has now become a rout.

There's more, seven earned runs of the stuff that swells my slender 1.96 earned run average to a pregnant 2.24, but I am into inflicting only so much pain when it is me who is doing the suffering.

By now, my wife knows me well enough to understand that it is best to let me grieve alone and Andrew, the three-year-old who has been excavating the unsodded back yard all afternoon, is too engrossed with mudpie production to appreciate the catastrophes a kids' game can inflict upon a grown-up who takes it all so seriously.

I lie down on the bed. I lace the fingers of my hands and settle them on my stomach. I close my eyes. All I need to complete the funeral arrangements is a bouquet of lilies, a bank of candles and a monkey to grind out the organ music.

It is at times like these, when I grow weary of such cheering thoughts as how long it would take to drown in a toilet bowl, that I wonder what kind of mind came up with the novel idea that eighteen men raising hell over a 5½-ounce baseball might keep the masses entertained through the sultry summer months.

You could lose the grip on your fastball just thinking about the many ways this game can test what passes for mental health these days.

It begins its eight-month love-hate relationship with its followers in the warmth of Florida, switches abruptly to snow and clammy rain in the north, staggers through the searing heat and cloying humidity of summer and, when everything is at stake, comes to climax when the frost is on the pumpkins. Its symmetry is so perfect—ninety feet between the bases, sixty feet, six inches from mound to plate, 330 feet to the nearest fences, 400 or more to the farthest—that most of the outs are made by a matter of inches. It is a game that brings out the best and the worst in the individual, yet it must be played collectively or not at all. And, perhaps a question only a pitcher could ask, in what other game in this part of the world does the defence start out with the ball?

Were it not for the fact that it draws upon so wide an assortment of characters—geez, if they're here I can't be so nuts after all—I would worry. Maybe Graig Nettles, with the New York Yankees at the time and speaking of a specific situation, said it best for all of us: "When I was a kid, I had two ambitions. To be a ballplayer or perform in the circus. Here, I get to do both."

From the ice fields of Alaska, from the swampland of Mississippi, from the Texas Panhandle, the mountains of Mexico and the swarming streets of villages in South America, they are drawn by God knows what consuming passion to play this game. Believe me, it is more than fame, fortune and a ton of fun. Cracking safes has to be easier, the hours are definitely better and there's no problem waking up with jet lag, or worse, in a strange hotel room.

Within this collection of misfits, whose common bond is the color and stripe of their uniforms, there is no breed further apart than the starting pitcher and the so-called position player.

Let us begin by examining the work ethic that binds each to his toil.

I'm not saying pitchers work any harder in spring but, since they generally report a week to ten days earlier, it's a fact that they work longer. Sure, since the wear on their arms is a mite more pronounced, they spend a few more afternoons on the golf course later on when the games begin and they're not scheduled for duty, but you get the message.

Depending on the pitching rotation his manager has set up, the starter works every fourth or fifth day. Unless he falters, which is often enough, he is expected to put his all—every ounce of energy, every facet of the craft he has been honing since childhood, every particle of blind faith he can summon—into every one of the 125 pitches he hopes to make that day. Every one of them is judged by an umpire and, on every one, there is a winner and a loser. Mix in a few well-directed hits on a bad day and it is bound to take a toll on a guy's sense of self-esteem.

Fail ultimately and, in full view of the thousands who have paid good money to see him succeed, his manager strolls out to the mound and plucks the ball from his hand. It goes with the territory. I realize that, but there is no ceremony in any other sport that quite compares with it for sheer embarrassment.

I'm not saying either that the fielders are nodding off while I'm busting a gut making good pitches. Far from it, but on the busiest afternoon they might handle ten chances. I agree, too, that the designated hitter relieves me of the task of taking a bat in my hands and facing about fifteen pitches but, by the same token, it means four fewer easy outs for me.

When a hitter fails miserably, his salvation is most likely at hand the next day. His three-day slump makes for a dreary weekend, but the starter who goes into the tank three times running is doomed to a hellish couple of weeks wondering when the next milk train pulls out for Syracuse. (There were times earlier this season, I must admit, when a couple of weeks in upstate New York didn't look all that bad.)

Take the collar, 0-for-5, in an afternoon, and no doubt the hitter has a few more in the lineup to accompany him in his misery. The pitcher, whether he died by his own hand or was done in by the misdeeds of others, stands alone in defeat. It's on his record, in the big book forever, and nothing will ever bring it back. Say it isn't so, especially after a season in which my own mark was 14–13 in spite of the league's best ERA at 2.48.

Even the standards for perfection are different.

The hitter who goes 5-for-5 might have punched holes in the fence all afternoon or, as is more likely, a couple of his hits were strictly from the sandlots. Just the same, his performance goes into the books as a perfect day at the plate.

There's an argument to be made, I'll admit, that a pitcher can give up a hit to the leadoff batter every inning, walk the next two men, and nine hits and eighteen walks later, be a 1–0 winner with a miracle or three on his behalf. The point is, even if I can't trot out sixty feet, six inches of stats to back it up, that pitching is the tougher proposition. Physically as well as mentally.

The hitter whose average is .300 (a .700 failure rate) will drive a Caddy, drink soda pop until his spikes rot and marry a dishy blonde. The pitcher who wins as many as he loses, a .500 success (failure) rate, is flirting with mediocrity. And there's nothing in the statistics to say what kind of support, good or bad, he was given at the plate or in the field. The earned run average is a little more accurate but it, too, has its flaws. Is his home field, where the pitcher makes half of his starts, a haven for hitters or the next best thing to the Grand Canyon? Are the fielders behind him gifted with quick feet and soft hands or are their legs made of lead and their gloves of granite?

Perfection? For a pitcher it is the standard with which he

must enter every game, yet know that his is an art of compromise once the first pitch is sent on its way. It is the ability to con oneself that two, four, six or a dozen hits does not a shabby outing make if the team won. Perfection? It is attained once every game, but only because the batter and his friend, the umpire, are not allowed in the bullpen.

In the final analysis, there is but one legitimate judge of a pitcher's worth. He has been there when every pitch was made. He is supremely aware of every nuance of cunning, every ounce of care and pain that went into them. He alone saw at first hand what became of them, what caprices of fate and questionable calls robbed him of his due.

Now if only a pitcher could learn to be impartial.

Don't get me wrong. I've had my share of luck on pitches that should have ended up in the Milky Way. And maybe I deserved to do time for conspiracy to assault when a few brave outfielders rubbed up against a few fences while tracking down my mistakes. Luck? Why one night in Minneapolis a couple of seasons back, I was let off the hook for a loss after the last out had been called.

We're down a run in the ninth, men on first and second with one out, reliever Ron Davis and Dave Engle the Twins' battery. Ground ball to second for one, relay to Kent Hrbek at first for two. The ump's arm goes up, but the ball pops out of Hrbek's glove. Safe. As pinch-runner Mitch Webster tears around third, Hrbek scoops up the ball and fires to home. By this time, Engle is halfway to the mound, his hand out to congratulate an amazed Davis, as Webster and the ball cross the plate. Our bullpen wins it in extra innings and, like I say, I'm a winner if only because I'm not a loser.

It happens now and then, I admit, but—and maybe I'm still feeling the effects of the debacle against Texas—not often enough to tip the scales of pitching justice.

If there is one thing that helps me keep my equilibrium, such as it might be, it is the understanding that there is precious little I can do once I let go of the ball. Another thing that helps me is my rule that what I do at the ballpark stays at the ballpark the minute I walk out the clubhouse door. I am reminded of the saying attributed to Yogi Berra, but which most folks only get half-right: "It ain't over till it's over . . . but when it's over, it's over."

Easy to say, I tell myself as the shadows slip across the ceiling and drench the bedroom in a comforting blackness. Then there's a knock on the door and three-year-old Andrew, king of the sandcastles, chef supreme of the mudpie makers, pops in to tell his daddy that dinner is getting cold. He's as happy as a lark to see me.

Texas? Where's Texas?

Great Dame

She's nearly 80 and needs a touch of paint
but my heart belongs to this old girl

SHE IS 347 DOWN THE LINES, sweeps out another 35 feet or so in the alleys and is 409 to dead center. If Comiskey Park were a woman, she'd be pinned up on the crossbeam of every pitcher's locker in the American League.

Who cares that the old girl has been around for nearly eighty years or that, save for a couple of tucks a few years back to satisfy the hitters and a touch of paint for her admirers, the lady's face has remained the same since the time of Ty Cobb, Tris Speaker and G.H. Ruth.

Grand dame of ballparks she might be, but I consider her as being positively voluptuous. If I throw another 50,000 pitches, I'll never find a park so faithful to history and, even after all these years, so right for a pitcher.

That's what I thought the first time I saw her, as a rookie called up midway through the '79 season. That's what I thought the day I pitched my first shutout there in my rookie year and, one Saturday in August last year, the night I came within three outs of pitching the club's first no-hitter.

161

Dammit. It was so close.

Until Rudy Law planted my first pitch of the ninth inning a couple of rows into the seats in right field, I thought for sure it was mine. He hit a fastball, which I had every intention of leaving high and outside, a pitch he had beaten into the ground the other three times he came to the plate that night. The instant replay later surprised me when it showed my most critical pitch of the night cutting the heart of the plate. My grandmother, God bless her, could have ridden it downtown.

As soon as Law hit this one, I knew any hope of becoming a part of Comiskey Park's lore would have to wait for another day. It was great fun while it lasted, but I'd be lying if I said I wasn't a little disappointed. To be honest, though, I was anything but devastated. I figure I came at Law with the best I had and, on this one pitch, he was better. That I had nothing left to give was apparent a few pitches later when Bryan Little, a .250 hitter, parked another fastball, this one not so good either, in the same section of seats.

Thinking back on it, I'd have to say it would have ranked among the weirdest scenarios for a no-hitter or near no-hitter. Usually, when a guy comes close, there have been a few sparkling plays behind him. Until the ninth, I can't remember anything but routine outs and the one error, groan, committed by a pitcher alleged to have a sure set of hands.

Nor were there any premonitions.

A no-hitter was the farthest thing from my mind when I boarded the team bus that afternoon for the park. And, if you can believe it, farther still while I warmed up in the bullpen.

Blame that part of it on the Windy City.

We had been told the game, due to get under way at 6 p.m., would be delayed a couple of hours by some rough weather coming off Lake Michigan. At about 5:30, trainer Ken Carson created instant panic when he told me we'd be going on time.

Had I known, I would have been dressed half an hour before, would have done my twenty-five minutes of stretching exercises and, at this point, would just now be flopping on the trainer's table to have my arm rubbed down.

Suffice to say that fifteen minutes before the first pitch, I was getting my rubdown . . . in the bullpen. Luckily, the slider was on the mark and the fastball was behaving. The curve was nothing special and the changeup, as usual, was all over the place. I've won with less, lots less, so I was thankful for what I had when I trotted out to pitch the first inning.

Thoughts of a no-hitter? Not yet. Like the groom who stayed too long at his own stag, I was more worried about getting to the church on time. In any case, painful experience has taught me to be suspicious the nine or ten times a season when my bullpen stuff is so fine I could set down Murderer's Row on nine pitches. That's usually the day Skid Row sends you to the showers around the third inning.

If I had to choose, in fact, I would prefer good control over good material. The former will get you out of more tight spots than the latter. When I do pitch a no-hitter, odds are it'll be with stuff that's less than exceptional and luck that is more than exceptional.

While historical thoughts were the farthest thing from my mind as I rushed to get ready, it didn't take long to get in the mood.

Don't let anybody kid you. Like any other pitcher in the major leagues, thoughts of immortality crossed my mind as soon as I put away Law, Little and Harold Baines 1-2-3 in the White Sox half of the first. Nothing I was taking too seriously, mind you, but the temptation was there. Anybody who says it isn't is either a confirmed pessimist or doesn't have enough faith in himself. In either case, careers in the major leagues tend to be short.

I buried the thought, more or less, until I came back to the dugout after the third inning. Nine up, nine down. Look, up on the scoreboard . . .

	1 2 3		R H E
White Sox	0 0 0		0 0 0

Nothing to get excited about, considering the way the dugouts were built at Comiskey Park, with your 1910 midget model of ballplayer in mind. The cement ceilings are low and many a modern-day player has taken his lumps when the heat of the moment gave him a case of the jumps. Not me. Not yet.

Around the sixth, as had been the custom since spring training, my arm started getting tight and I tried to ignore it. Pitching through pain is no big deal and, in this instance, they could have amputated between innings and I would have gone out there and tossed left-handed. It is something I can do, by the way, so long as I stick with the slow-w-w-w changeup.

With a number of near-misses on my record, I knew better than to get ahead of myself.

The summer before in Oakland, I survived into the seventh inning, coughed up a home run with one out, but hung on to win the game 2–1 in the tenth. In June of '83 at Tiger Stadium, Larry Herndon broke up another bid with a single in the seventh. My shutout lasted until the ninth when I got the hook after a walk and two singles filled the bases. Lance Parrish doubled home three runs off Randy Moffitt and Rick Leach tied it with a single off Joey McLaughlin. We won it in the tenth. Manager Bobby Cox was so certain I would do it in September of '82 at Oakland that he replaced left fielder Al Woods with Barry Bonnell for defensive purposes in the seventh inning. Bonnell arrived just in time to watch a blast by Tony Armas soar over his head and deep into the seats.

When I made it through the seventh at Chicago, just to assure myself of what was happening, I took another look at the scoreboard. There it was . . .

	1 2 3	4 5 6	7	R H E
White Sox	0 0 0	0 0 0	0	0 0 0

That's when I began letting go of the cautious side of my

nature. Make it through eight, I told myself, and you've got a good shot at it.

Sure, I knew I was on the threshold of history. So did the other twenty-four players on the bench. So did Coxie, coaches Al Widmar, Cito Gaston, Billy Smith, John Sullivan and Jimy Williams. So did the trainers, the equipment manager, batboy and any mice who might have been hiding beneath the dugout floorboards.

Not one of them dared mention it. Usually during a game, while you might not get into any extended conversation, the odd comment is exchanged. Not tonight. Not a word. From anybody.

Superstitious? Everybody knows ballplayers aren't superstititous. For instance, I attribute it to mere coincidence that, as I did that day, I now eat a tuna fish sandwich, toasted on whole wheat, before each starting assignment in Chicago. But that's a ritual and it will last forever or until my luck there goes sour.

I took it as a good omen that, after we had sent nine men to the plate and scored three runs for a 6–0 cushion in the top of the eighth, my half of the inning was a breeze. Three up, three down, minimum amount of pitches. Law, Little and Baines to go, just like the first inning.

First, however, I had to battle myself.

The spot beneath my elbow was throbbing and on the first couple of soft tosses as I warmed up for the ninth, pain shot the length of my arm. To get through the inning, I told myself, I had to get something on my pitches. By the time I completed my warmups, six more pitches, I figured a decent fastball would do the job.

Either it didn't have enough on it, which was true to some degree, or Law was waiting for it. As soon as he hit it, I knew my no-hitter was gone. Little's home run, three pitches later, told me I had nothing left. Coxie came out with the hook and our bullpen put away a 6–3 victory.

Believe me when I say I was only a little let down when

Law parked that first pitch and Little added the exclamation point.

Odd, isn't it, that after eight more or less perfect innings, without anything close to a hit, I go to the opposite extreme by giving up two home runs. I would have been happier by far had they smacked two sharp singles and allowed me a shutout. Hanging the collar that night on Tom Seaver, who has done all the things I'd like to do and was still battling the hitters at the age of forty, would have been reason enough to be proud.

More important, now that I think back on it, was that I had given it my best and, when it was not to be, I showed myself I could rise above it. Well aware of how I might have handled it when I had less of that precious commodity known as composure—ask Buck Martinez how maturely I behaved when Bull Luzinski beat me with a three-run homer here in May of '82—I had to consider that a victory in itself.

In situations like this one, it's second nature for a pitcher to second-guess himself.

I had been so satisfied in the bullpen with my slider, which was exceptional, and fastball, which was good, that I hadn't thrown a curve or a changeup for eight innings. I could have tried being cute, tried the soft stuff on Law, but I would have been really miffed with myself had he beaten me on anything but what I thought was my best.

I cancelled my own ticket for a perfect game in the fourth inning by botching Little's bunt to my left. I should have waited for it to take another bounce, but I decided to go right at it. After knocking it down, I gave it a hurried backhand flip when I should have taken my time and picked up the ball cleanly. Then I threw it away for a two-base error. If I'd had a mirror in my hip pocket, I would have whipped it out and glared at myself for making such a bonehead play. By saving the pitches I had to make to an extra batter, would I have had a few more miles, or better location, on the fastball Law lined into the seats?

Never would I suggest that a team scoring three runs on my behalf is doing anything but a great service—as things turned out, it was the margin of victory—but did the long wait in the eighth inning exact its toll on my arm?

Who knows? Who'll ever know?

What I do know is that it was fun while it lasted and that, one day, I'll be there again.

Omens

After the season of despair I had in '86
I looked for hope anywhere I could find it

TIME TO GO HOME . . .

The Bronco had been packed to its rafters for the trip to Florida. The tank had been filled, the oil changed, the tires checked at the gas station around the corner the night before. The first chords from Geddy Lee's guitar were throbbing from the tape deck into which I had just slipped my favorite *Rush* tape.

So why was I stuck in the driveway, staring at the brass numbers *1881* on the front porch of my summer home in Toronto?

After a season where my W-L record plunged to 7-12, my ERA soared to 4.74 and my confidence had taken the worst hammering since the Indians shut out Custer at the Little Big Horn, I was ready for an omen.

OK, my W-L mark would go to 18-8 in '87 and we'd end up Number 1. "I'll take it," I said. Or my ERA would sink to 1.88. "Cy Young numbers there." Or maybe, now that the pessimist (realist?) reached for control, that's how many miles I'll pile up before the van rolled to the door in Palm Harbor.

And then it dawned on me.

Hell, that's the number of major league innings I've put on my arm (regular season and playoff) since I joined the Blue Jays in Baltimore the evening of June 26, 1979, and —despite my best intentions—took a 6-1 pounding from the Orioles.

No wonder I was tired.

Aside from the accumulated mileage, it had been a long, long season for the pitcher who began it with visions (delusions?) of 20 victories dancing in his head and a club that figured to get even after it had been jobbed out of its World Series (winners) share. The team to beat in the American League East Division race last spring finished fourth with an 86–76 record, 9½ games back of the Boston Red Sox. The guy with the league-leading 2.48 ERA in '85—even if his 14-13 record did not fairly reflect it—could claim no such irony in a 7-12 record and 4.74 ERA.

Want more?

In 205 innings pitched, 50 to 75 fewer than the previous four seasons, I led the mound staff in giving up hits (239), walks (87) and home runs (29). At 127, my strikeouts were down anywhere from 40 to 70 from the previous three years.

I did record my first (and only) save in nine seasons as a pro but the real relief in mowing down four Seattle Mariners to preserve a 6-2 lead that July afternoon was that I did not blow Jim Clancy's 99th victory as a Blue Jay. The thought would not have entered his mind but, since we both wanted to be the first to hit the century mark, I can only guess at the howl I would have caused had I blown it.

Thank heaven for small mercies.

Look hard, I suppose, and what good came from this season of non-seasons for me was summed up in one short paragraph in a small story towards the back of the *Toronto Sun*

sports section a couple of days after our season ended. My
3-2 record (2.45 ERA over my last seven starts) for September, a month we began with soaring hopes only 3½ games
behind the Red Sox, earned me pitcher-of-the-month honors.

How did it ever get this crazy?

Had I lost it? Were my best days, as few as they might
have been, behind me? Was I done?

These were the questions—No! No! No again! were the
right answers to them, I kept telling myself—that clouded
every waking moment of every day of the longest, hottest
and most unsettled summer of my life.

I asked these questions at breakfast with the family huddled
over flapjacks at the kitchen table; in the Bronco, music
thumping from the tape deck, on the way to the ballpark; as
I sorted the suits of yet another clubhouse hand of hearts;
and, yes, as I watched clips of the young Roger Clemens
racking up another dozen Ks on the sportscast late at night.

When would it end? Would it ever end?

In the beginning, with all those high hopes from the '85
season waiting to be fulfilled, I thought my problems would
vanish in the dust of a couple of starts. Here it was the middle of October, a time when talent like ours should have been
tearing a strip off the World Series, and we were watching a
couple of other teams lunge for the brass ring.

You think I don't know we would have been there had I
lived up to my own high expectations and won the 20 games,
that magic mark I expect to achieve every season? To be sure, I
heard all the whispers and the one that hurt most is that $success
spoiled David Andrew Stieb. Yes, I made my million dollars last season and I'll make it again this summer, but you
wouldn't have to spend two weeks in George Steinbrenner's
shipyard to know that money does not necessarily buy baseball happiness. As easy to take as all that loot had been in
other seasons, I considered it much less of a bargain each
time I headed for the bank last summer.

What made it all the more frustrating for me was that if anything could go wrong when I was out there, it usually did.

Seeing-eye singles. Bullets that ricocheted off infielders' gloves. Bloopers. Bleeders. Tweeners. Jam shots. Lazy flies that outfielders lost in the glare of the sun off the screen behind home plate.

With a full moon in its ascendancy over Arlington Stadium one sweaty Friday night early last August, the ridiculous became the insane during an outing against the Texas Rangers.

If there have been three more disastrous innings of work chalked up against my name, I do not remember them and, furthermore, I would not look kindly upon the person who did. Among my indiscretions that night were: giving up a pair of two-run home runs; two (quick) wild pitches that allowed Larry Parrish to trot home after he had doubled in the second inning; a sloppy throw past Willie Upshaw after a nice fielding play on a bunt in the third; nicking Pete Incaviglia with a pitch.

And that wasn't the worst of it.

As I walked across the third-base line toward our dugout at the end of the third inning, I looked out of the corner of my eye at umpire Steve Palermo and flicked the fingers of my right hand across the top of my knee to suggest, ever so politely, that he had not been calling the low strikes.

It might have been the heat, the full moon or something Palermo ate—normally, like all umpires, he is a man of even temper—but that night he blew a gasket. In a flash, he was in our dugout and cussing me all the way back to my Teutonic ancestors. Though we were separated by a dozen of my teammates and coaches, he found in me a willing accomplice for a debate over exactly what kind of canine brought each of us into this world.

It ended with Stieb and manager Jimy Williams getting tossed out of the game—me for the first time in my career; my boss for the third time that season.

And they call *me* a hothead.

If, as they say, luck has a way of balancing out, I will have retired from baseball by the time you read this—having broken the bank over the winter at the jai-alai courts in Tampa. If, on the other hand, you see Number 37 back at his old stand on Opening Day this April, take it for granted that my competitive edge is as sharp as it can be and, the fates willing, I still have a flame of a fastball and a temper to match it.

Maybe it is true, after so much media fuss has been made of my tantrums on and off the mound, that I was a much nicer guy to be around last season. Maybe I was too nice. Reggie Jackson, late of the California Angels, for one, and George Bell of the Blue Jays, for another, were among the many who wanted to see more of Mr. Mean. If it works, I have concluded, then I suggest keeping the little ones far from the TV set the next time the camera zooms in on my pantomime after yet another seeing-eye, blooper, broken-bat tweener falls in for a @#%&*¢ hit.

If I tended to be a bit reserved last season, in and out of the clubhouse, it was because pitchers with records like mine —no matter how much they consider shabby luck to have played a part—are wise to be seldom seen and heard even less. Let me make my run at 20 this season and no one will be safe from this graduate of the caveman school of subtle wit.

Pardon me if this sounds like I'm reaching—it's an occupational hazard for pitchers—but there is a set of statistics that suggest to me that part of my problems last year might be attributable to long-term fatigue.

Call it *the Burnout Factor*. It goes back, if you want to stretch a point, to the numbers on the front porch that so fascinated me the day I pointed the Bronco to my winter home.

Battle fatigue, I discovered one afternoon while leafing through *The Baseball Encyclopedia*, seems to set in between 1,600 and 1,800 innings of a majority of the finest pitchers' careers. Following the most discouraging season of what ought to have been their prime, they often bounce back with some of their best years.

You could look it up. . .

■ Former Jay Doyle Alexander, after 1,746⅔ innings, was 1-7 (6.08 ERA) for the '82 Yankees and, in a fit of frustration with which I can identify, broke his hand smashing a dugout wall. He lost eight in a row in '83, six with us, then won seven straight. He was 17-6 (3.13) and 17-10 (3.45) the next two seasons.

■ After 1,327⅓ innings (in addition to pitching winter ball in the Dominican Republic) Joaquin Andujar followed a 6-16 (4.16) season for St. Louis in '83 with 20-14 (3.34) and 21-12 (3.40) campaigns.

■ Bob Gibson, after 1,726⅓ innings, dipped from 21-12 (2.44) with the '66 Cards to 13-7 (2.98)—pretty fine, admittedly, but still the fewest victories in the dozen years that made up his prime. He was 22-9 (1.12), 20-13 (2.18) and 23-7 (3.12) the next three seasons.

■ Steve Carlton, after 1,611 innings and a 27-10 (1.97) year with the '72 Phillies, fell to 13-20 (3.90). Over the next 10 seasons, he won close to 160 games.

■ Ferguson Jenkins, after 1,743 innings, plunged from 20-12 (3.21) for the '72 Cubs to 14-16 (3.89). He was 25-12 (2.83) with the Texas Rangers in '74.

■ Tom Seaver, after 1,931 innings with the Mets, went from 19-10 (2.08) in '73 to 11-11 (3.20) in '74. He was 22-9 (2.38) the next season and has won close to 150 games since to earn a pass into the Hall of Fame at Cooperstown.

Among others, similar cases can be made for Warren Spahn (363-245, 3.09), Jim Palmer (268-152, 2.86), Juan Marichal (243-142, 2.89) and Nolan Ryan (253-226, 3.15). After 1,654 innings and an '85 season in which I was 14-13 (2.48), I flatter myself by saying that my swoon in '86 at least has set the stage for matching their post-burnout performances.

At the same time, I concede that figures tend to lie, that liars tend to figure and that baseball is a breeding ground for both activities.

My difficulties last season began as early as my final outing in spring training, a seven-inning tuneup against our Triple A squad in Dunedin while the rest of the team played the Yankees at Fort Lauderdale.

Throughout the previous season, a group of flexor muscles near my right elbow had been acting up—a nuisance I take great pains (bad joke) in detailing elsewhere in these memoirs. A winter of rest and light exercise had cured the problem, I was sure, but it flared anew just in time for the season opener against the Rangers. I was anything but sharp, giving up five runs on six hits before I got the hook in the fifth in what became a 6-3 loss.

Then the tinkering began.

Pitching coach Al Widmar suggested the four walks I gave up were caused by a failure to open my stride to the plate. By landing a little more towards first base, my balance (and location) would improve.

Trouble was I began opening up too much, rushing my body ahead of my arm, when most of my weight went left instead of towards home.

I had to drop my arm a little on the delivery. I wasn't following through. My slider didn't bite. My curve was flat. My fastball had lost its snap.

All the while I was working on half a dozen elements of my delivery, I was trying to retire major league hitters.

Good luck.

Instead of throwing 110 tidy pitches through nine innings, the norm when my game goes my way, I was struggling with 100 through five innings.

Like a pebble tossed into a pond, there is a rippling effect.

It is no accident that defence is much sharper when it is kept on its toes by a pitcher throwing strikes. With the increased likelihood of having to make a play, they have to be more alert. Your own hitters are affected, too, because they are more relaxed at the plate if they believe you can hold a lead and they don't have to swing for the fences in hopes of building the big inning to keep the team close.

Whatever the cause of my problems (some joker in the press box even suggested I start wearing a protective cup again) too often the effect was that I was more concerned with how the ball got to the plate than where it was when it crossed it.

As my troubles mounted—remember, it took all of two months to win my first game—what was left of my celebrated confidence rose and fell with the outcome of a given pitch.

Sure, it would be convenient to blame mine and other pitchers' problems last season on the secret switch to rabbit hide on the baseballs we were using, but that would suggest that Jesse Barfield and George Bell were less than full measure for the fireworks factory they founded by the shores of Lake Ontario last summer.

At the same time, I hope the builders of the new dome in Toronto are a little more conscious of space than the folks who renovated the telephone booth where we play our home games now. Real grass, too, would help the ERAs and, more important, prolong the careers of outfielders whose frames take an awful pounding on a field of synthetic turf that, in reality, feels something like a thick rug laid over a parking lot.

Over the seasons, I have been told that when it comes to winning, believing you have good stuff is almost as important as having it. Now I understand.

That confidence is king was driven home on our road trip to the west coast late in the summer. As I warmed up in the bullpen at Anaheim, I knew I had nothing to take into the game against the California Angels. No fastball. No slider. No curve. I was history by the fourth inning, behind 5-2 on three unearned runs in a game we went on to lose 9-3.

As I prepared for the Royals ten days later, I had stuff that would have won me twenty games had I been able to bring it into every one of my thirty-four starts. The fastball darted. The curve changed lanes. The slider careened like a car on a patch of ice. And all of them were shaving that little black ribbon around the plate where hitters fear to tread. Through seven innings, I gave up four hits and left a 5-1 lead in the capable hands of relievers Mark Eichhorn and Tom Henke.

It may be true that what you have in the bullpen has no bearing on what you take into the game—all manner of magic or mayhem can shape a game plan in that 150-foot march to the mound—but with the past performances I took with me into battle, what I saw in the bullpen was what I had going for me.

When it's not there, you can guess what I'm thinking as I take that long walk to the mound to face somebody with a bat in his hands.

Confidence. You can't see it, touch it, smell it—but it has to be there for anyone to be successful in any walk (ugh, there's that word again) of life. I often wished, by the power of positive thinking, I could ignore all that had gone on before and summon that sense of invincibility I all but considered part of my equipment in other years.

A magician I am not. Until I do master the black arts, like other humans I will have to settle for the fruits of sweat, toil and tears to provide me with the sense of well-being or otherwise that I take into a game.

As volatile as these swings in emotion can be, it should come as no shock that if I never get the opportunity to record my second save, it will be too soon. Never mind that I was shelled my first time out last season, or that I was nibbled to death the third time, it's the uncertainty of the profession that reduces me to a wreck.

You know neither when, nor if, the manager will stroll from the dugout and crook a finger in your direction, caring not a stream of spit whether your psyche is as high as a kite or as low as whale droppings.

Like my second time out, when I saved Clancy's 99th as a Blue Jay. Anyone who follows our fortunes is aware we both wanted to be the first to win 100 and that I was considered a cinch to do it at the start of the season.

Had I blown it for Clancy, I would have run myself out of Seattle on a monorail. Believe me when I say I was happier than I should have been when I put Clancy within one of the magic mark.

What my short, unhappy life as a fireman did teach me is a valuable lesson in energy conservation. I found I wasted far too much of that precious commodity warming up for starts. Usually, I toss about 60 pitches but there was nowhere near that time available in a relief situation. I found I was just as fluid after 25 to 30 or, depending on the humidity, even fewer pitches.

Perhaps the greatest lessons I learned in my summer of discontent were the ones taught to me off the field. I think back to younger days and how poorly I would have coped with the type of adversity I faced. I'm sure you've heard of me glaring at errant infielders, breaking up clubhouse furniture, mean-mouthing the newspaper guys, and tipping bar-keeps a nickel.

Make no mistake, I feel just as sorely these days when things go wrong. It's just that I have devised different ways of dealing with it.

When you have a place called home and a family waiting —a wife who rides the same roller-coaster of emotions, but who cannot help me once I cross those white lines; and a couple of toddlers who have no idea that grown men can get so serious about a child's game—reality has a way of putting the surreal into perspective.

The letters from the fans that arrived each day at my winter home, the vast majority supportive, tell me I am right to believe that things will turn out right. Can that many people be wrong?

When—not if—I do right myself, I will be the first to see that they take their share of the credit.

Like I keep telling myself: tomorrow I'll be perfect.

DAVID ANDREW STIEB

Name pronounced Steeb

(Dave)

Born July 22, 1957, at Santa Ana, Calif.

Height, 6.01. Weight 185.

Throws and bats righthanded.

Attended Santa Ana College, Santa Ana, Calif., and
Southern Illinois University, Carbondale, Ill.

Brother of Steve Stieb, catcher in Atlanta Braves' organization, 1979 through 1981.

YEAR	CLUB	LEAGUE	G	IP	W	L	Pct.	GS	CG	SHO	SV	H	R	ER	SO	BB	HB	WP	ERA
1978—	Dunedin	Florida St.	4	26	2	0	1.000	4	1	0	0	23	10	6	8	1	0	0	2.08
1979—	Dunedin	Florida St.	8	51	5	0	1.000	8	2	1	0	54	30	24	38	28	4	3	4.24
1979—	Syracuse	Int'national	7	51	5	2	.714	7	4	0	0	39	15	12	20	14	2	1	2.12
1979—	Toronto	American	18	129	8	8	.500	18	7	1	0	139	70	62	52	48	4	3	4.33
1980—	Toronto†	American	34	243	12	15	.444	32	14	4	0	232	108	100	108	83	4	6	3.70
1981—	Toronto	American	25	184	11	10	.524	25	11	2	0	148	70	65	89	61	‡11	6	3.18
1982—	Toronto	American	38	288⅓	17	14	.548	38	*19	*5	0	271	116	104	141	75	5	3	3.25
1983—	Toronto	American	36	278	17	12	.586	36	14	4	0	223	105	94	187	93	*14	5	3.04
1984—	Toronto	American	35	267	16	8	.667	35	11	2	0	215	87	84	198	88	*11	2	2.83
1985—	Toronto	American	36	265	14	13	.519	36	8	2	0	206	89	73	167	96	9	4	*2.48
Major League Totals—7 Years			222	1654⅓	95	80	.543	220	84	20	0	1434	645	582	942	544	60	24	3.17

Selected by Toronto Blue Jays' organization in 5th round of free-agent draft, June 6, 1978.

†Appeared in one game as outfielder with no chances.

*Best in the league.

‡Tied for Best in the league

CHAMPIONSHIP SERIES RECORD

Established Championship Series record for most games started, Series (3), 1985
Established American League Championship Series records for most innings pitched (20⅓),
most bases on balls (10) and most strikeouts (18), seven-game Series, 1985.

YEAR	CLUB	LEAGUE	G	IP	W	L	Pct.	GS	CG	SHO	SV	H	R	ER	SO	BB	HB	WP	ERA
1985—	Toronto	... American	3	20⅓	1	1	.500	3	0	0	0	11	7	7	18	10	1	0	3.10

ALL-STAR GAME RECORD

Tied All-Star Game record for most wild pitches, inning and game (2), July 8, 1980 (seventh inning).

YEAR	LEAGUE	IP	W	L	Pct.	GS	CG	SHO	SV	H	R	ER	SO	BB	HB	WP	ERA
1980—	American	1	0	0	.000	0	0	0	0	1	1	0	0	2	2	2	0.00
1981—	American	1⅔	0	0	.000	0	0	0	0	1	0	0	1	1	1	0	0.00
1983—	American	3	1	0	1.000	1	0	0	0	0	1	0	4	1	0	0	0.00
1984—	American	2	0	1	.000	1	0	0	0	3	2	1	2	0	0	0	4.50
1985—	American	1	0	0	.000	0	0	0	0	0	0	0	2	1	0	0	0.00
All-Star Game Totals—5 Years		8⅔	1	1	.500	2	0	0	0	5	4	1	9	5	3	2	1.04

RECORD AS OUTFIELDER

YEAR	CLUB	LEAGUE	Pos.	G	AB	R	H	2B	3B	HR	RBI	BA	PO	A	E	FA
1978—	Dunedin	.. Florida St.	OF-P	35	99	10	19	3	0	1	9	.192	85	7	3	.968

STIEB'S BEST
SEASON

W	17 — 1982-83
ERA	2.48 — 1985
IP	288.1 — 1982
SO	198 — 1984
Win Strk	5 — 1979, '83-84

GAME

Low Hit	2 vs Bost. 8/10/82
SO	11 at Minn. 8/26/84
	vs Det. 9/4/83

Dave Stieb vs AMERICAN LEAGUE
CAREER

	ERA	W	L	G	IP	H	ER
TOTALS	3.17	95	80	222	1654.0	1434	582
HOME	3.39	49	41	104	783.1	713	295
ROAD	2.97	46	39	118	870.2	721	287
vs BALT	3.70	3	7	18	116.2	100	48
BOST	4.57	3	7	17	106.1	105	54
CALF	2.82	8	4	17	127.2	102	40
CHGO	1.86	12	3	16	130.1	82	27
CLEV	2.89	7	6	16	124.2	114	40
DET	3.58	6	8	17	120.2	134	48
KC	2.99	8	7	17	135.1	117	45
MILW	2.94	10	5	18	144.0	131	47
MINN	2.83	5	9	18	143.1	123	45
NY	2.96	5	8	19	142.2	118	47
OAK	3.58	7	6	16	120.2	114	48
SEA	3.22	11	4	16	117.1	101	42
TEX	3.69	8	6	17	124.1	114	51

Dave Stieb vs AMERICAN LEAGUE
1985 SEASON

	ERA	W	L	G	IP	H	ER
TOTALS	2.48	14	13	36	265.0	206	73
HOME	2.96	8	6	15	112.1	104	37
ROAD	2.12	6	7	21	152.2	102	36
vs BALT	1.93	0	0	2	14.0	10	3
BOST	2.84	1	1	2	12,2	13	4
CALF	1.44	1	1	3	25.0	16	4
CHGO	0.75	3	0	3	24.0	3	2
CLEV	4.15	1	2	3	21.2	24	10
DET	1.57	2	1	3	23.0	10	4
KC	2.70	0	3	3	23.1	21	7
MILW	1.44	1	2	3	25.0	20	4
MINN	2.95	0	1	3	21.1	16	7
NY	1.52	0	0	3	23.2	16	4
OAK	3.86	1	1	2	14.0	18	6
SEA	3.65	2	0	2	12.1	11	5
TEX	4.68	2	1	4	25.0	23	13
vs EAST	2.18	5	6	16	120.0	93	29
WEST	2.73	9	7	20	145.0	113	44
BEF ASG	1.87	9	5	20	144.2	98	30
AFT ASG	3.22	5	8	16	120.1	108	43
DAY	3.58	5	6	14	103.0	93	41
NIGHT	1.78	9	7	22	162.0	113	32
STARTER	2.48	14	13	36	265.0	206	73
in APR	2.93	1	2	5	30.2	27	10
MAY	1.69	4	1	6	42.2	27	8
JUNE	1.51	3	2	6	47.2	28	8
JULY	2.03	2	1	6	48.2	40	11
AUGUST	3.80	2	3	6	45.0	36	19
SEP/OCT	3.04	2	4	7	50.1	48	17

STRIKEOUT HIGH	8 — at Calf. May 2
	at NY June 12
	at Minn Aug. 28
WIN/LOSS STREAK	4/3
OPP BATTING AVERAGE	.213
SO per 9 INNINGS	5.67
BB per 9 INNINGS	3.26

1985 SEASON

	AB	H	HR	BB	SO	BA	SA	OBA
Leading Off Inn.	245	57	7	28	37	.233	.376	.319
Bases Empty	577	117	17	62	89	.203	.329	.287
Runners On	389	89	5	34	78	.229	.306	.294
Runners/Scor. Pos.	206	41	1	20	50	.199	.262	.274
Runners On/ 2 Out	157	30	1	12	37	.191	.236	.257
Scor. Pos./2 Out	97	18	1	6	27	.186	.258	.240
Late Inning Pressure	143	39	2	16	22	.273	.392	.350
Leading Off	38	7	0	4	7	.184	.263	.262
Bases Empty	85	19	2	8	13	.224	.365	.290
Runners On	58	20	0	8	9	.345	.431	.433
Runners/Scor. Pos.	33	14	0	6	5	.424	.576	.525
First 9 Batters	289	60	3	27	54	.208	.280	.287
Second 9 Batters	286	65	6	26	51	.227	.325	.293
All Batters Thereafter	391	81	13	43	62	.207	.345	.290